Lineland

*Mortality and Mercy on the Internet's
Pynchon-L@Waste.Org Discussion List*

THOMAS RUGGLES PYNCHON, JR.
AS HE MIGHT APPEAR IN 1997

Illustration from memory by Christine Wexler
Pencil on paper, 14 cm. by 21 cm.

Lineland

Mortality and Mercy on the Internet's Pynchon-L@Waste. Org Discussion List

By Jules Siegel, Christine Wexler, *et al.*

INTANGIBLE ASSETS MANUFACTURING

PHILADELPHIA

ISBN 1-885876-04-1

Library of Congress Catalog Card Number: 97-71389

"Who is Thomas Pynchon…And Why Is He Taking Off With My Wife"
originally appeared in *Playboy,* March, 1977

Typography and graphic design by JULES SIEGEL
𝓣𝒉𝒆 𝓒𝒐𝒎𝒎𝒖𝒏𝒊𝒄𝒂𝒕𝒊𝒐𝒏 𝓒𝒐𝒎𝒑𝒂𝒏𝒚
CANCUN, QUINTANA ROO, MEXICO

INTANGIBLE ASSETS MANUFACTURING
828 Ormond Avenue, Drexel Hill, PA 19026-2604
Web Site HTTP://WWW.IAM.COM *Email* INFO@IAM.COM

PRINTED IN THE UNITED STATES OF AMERICA
FIRST EDITION, FIRST PRINTING

Dedication
for JAMES AND MAE POPE

In Memoriam
CHESTER ANDERSON
1932–1991

Also by Jules Siegel

RECORD
Straight Arrow, 1972

THE YOUTH CULTURE
The Playboy Press, 1973

MEMOIR
The Mendocino Press, 1975

THE JOURNAL OF THE ABSURD
With Bernard Garfinkel
Workman Publishing, 1980

CANCUN: A BANKERS' FANTASY
Translated from the Spanish of Fernando Martí
Ediciones Martí, 1991

CANCUN USER'S GUIDE
with Anita Brown and Faera Siegel
The Communication Company, 1995

Contents

Preface   i
By Dale L. Larson

Introduction   viii
In which the author grants himself the customary indulgences.

Part 1: Vanity   1
In which our hero gets connected.

Part 2: A Lurker No More   35
A rousing welcome for the old guy.

Part 3: A Midnight Visit with the Werewolf   46
In which the old guy begins to howl.

Part 4: What did Lolita Say About Humbert?   69
Two characters talk about an author.

Part 5: Flame Wars   81
In which the situation begins to get out of hand.

Part 6: Manifestations of Venus   99
In which V. gets a folk job.

Part 7: Report Cards & Farewell   131
Our hero speaks his mind…and tries to say goodbye.

Epilogue: The Future of the Book of the Future   152

Appendix   158
Frequently Asked Questions

Index   165

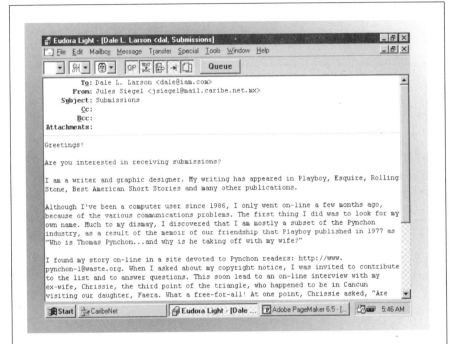

E-MAIL MESSAGE FROM JULES SIEGEL TO DALE L. LARSON
November 19, 1996

You are looking at the screen of a computer running the e-mail program Eudora Light under Windows 95. E-mail stands for electronic mail, which joins many millions of correspondents in a continuum of ongoing discussions with direct roots all the way back to Aristotle and Socrates.

Steve Dorner wrote Eudora in 1990 and named it for Eudora Welty, author of "Why I Live At the P.O." Eudora is freeware, a program given away free, partly because that's the Internet way, but also to promote a commercial version that has more advanced functions. The name is a classic example of Internet whimsy. Unix, the main Internet operating system, comes with a mail notification utility called Biff, supposedly because there was a dog named Biff who barked furiously whenever the postman arrived at the Berkeley, California, building in which a version of Unix was being programmed. —JULES SIEGEL

Preface

I'M WRITING THIS FROM A FUNKY CHEAP HOTEL ROOM IN COZUMEL, MEXICO. Under $14 a night, no TV or phone, irregular cracked and patchy cement walls and ceiling, the hand-made wood closet and bathroom door are unfinished or old or both. The floor is large aqua-blue tile, each with a slightly different pattern in white swirls. The room is reasonably clean, and the only bugs I've seen were small. I have a view of the ocean, but I'm not here on vacation. I've been meeting with Jules Siegel, who lives in the super-modern Cancun hotel zone, about thirty miles away by car and ferry. I'm at this hotel on Cozumel Island for two days of diving while he finishes some work on the manuscript, then I'll be back. Teo, Jules' Mexican friend, a diving instructor in Cancun, recommended this hotel. Staying here is helping me to understand all of this, to put it into perspective.

For the past fourteen years, Jules Siegel and his family have lived in an isolated land surrounded at once by both a booming resort town and by dense, dangerous jungle. During those same years, as a software-engineer-turned-publisher, I've lived much of my life in an electronic jungle with many of its own utopian elements. Our worlds came together only recently with the e-mail message shown on the facing page, which you see here as it appeared to Jules when he sent it. I use a different e-mail program, PINE (for Pine Is Not Elm—Elm being another program that Pine sort of grew out of), so it looked a bit different to me, but the message was the same.

My company, IAM, had just published its first non-computer book, *Torn Shapes of Desire: Internet Erotica* by Mary Anne Mohanraj. Jules found out about the book on the Web, and from it decided that IAM was a different kind of publisher, one which might really understand his new project and see the potential in it. He explained that most publishers are too stuck in an old idea of what a book *is*. Jules and I share some ideas about what books will be. The Internet is bringing about some of the new directions.

From the e-mail that followed, I learned that Jules wanted to put together a book having something to do with Thomas Pynchon and e-mail discussions about him. I said, "Who the hell is Thomas Pynchon?" It turns out that he's a famous reclusive author, though perhaps more popular among an older generation and among scholarly types. (If you really want to know more about who Thomas Pynchon is, feel free to skip ahead to page 83.) At first, I wasn't very interested, but Jules had an impressive background, and we talked more. Soon I realized that the book would be about much more than Thomas Pynchon. Jules was new to the net, and he was using it to reconnect to the world. The results, true to his form, were electric. I decided that I wanted to publish his book, and that I'd have to spend some time with him in Mexico to do it.

IN THE 1960S AND '70S, Jules Siegel had quite a successful literary and journalistic career in the United States. In addition to his four books, his works have appeared in *Playboy, Rolling Stone, The New York Times*, and many other publications. Though many of his friends became more famous, he achieved some measure of fame himself, and he did as much to shape the liberal thoughts of those times as he did to report them. Much of this book is about remembering those years, and explaining them to new generations.

Jules has lived his adult life as something of a nomad, and began living in Mexico in the early Seventies. He and his wife, Anita Brown, their newborn son, Eli, and his daughter Faera, then ten years old, left the United States on December 3, 1981 and landed in La Paz, Baja California Sur. They have not been back to the United States since. Jesse was born in Cancun in 1984.

Many Mexicans live a life not so different from our own. It isn't quaint. They have cars, air conditioning, TVs and VCRs. They may not have as many other possessions as their northern neighbors, but their culture is not as materialistic, and they don't always feel any poorer for it. While the working poor of the United States are much better off than the Mexican working poor, the middle class of the United States is not so different from the Mexican middle class. As a successful publicist and graphic designer in Mexico, Jules belonged to their upper middle class, enjoying a measure of success and living in one of Cancun's nicest neighborhoods. Paradoxically, he's also been living on the edge. One thing which distinguishes the Mexican middle-class is the economic upheavals of recent Mexican history. With the radical devaluations of the peso (many in the last two decades), a life savings can be destroyed overnight, and a lucrative work contract becomes worthless.

Many of Mexico's resources are still devoted to building roads and sanitation facilities and other basics. Phones aren't as important, both because of other priorities and because the culture is very much one of walking-around and of face-to-face meetings. Only one in ten Mexican homes has a telephone, and they aren't cheap. Newer technology like the Internet is even less widespread. Jules didn't have a telephone until November, 1996, although he has had a complete PC-based graphic design studio since 1989. "I used to be a telephone junkie" he told me. "I would run up huge long-distance bills and then scramble to pay them. When we moved to Mexico, I just left all that behind."

Before I came to visit, I asked if there was anything they'd like me to bring. The Siegel family asked for simple things that weren't available in Cancun. On their list were books, brown rice, beans, and other items which surprised me. I wasn't sure if they were joking, or living in extreme poverty, or if something else was going on. Before I left, I did go out and buy a suitcase full of gifts.

After I got to my hotel on Pok-Ta-Pok (an island surrounded by the lagoon formed by main the island of Cancun), I called Jules. His home and office were in separate units across the street in a condominium complex bordering the Cancun golf course, so he and Anita and oldest son Eli all came over and met me in the lobby. Jules is tall and slim, with wavy graying hair cut short, and round glasses with clear plastic frames. (Though I thought they were fashionably modern, I was later told that these are the same style glasses he's worn for more than fifty years.) He had a day or two's growth of white stubble and was wearing a dark cranberry T-shirt and comfortable worn jeans. His face had a character most women would find appealing, more so for the ridges and furrows which have developed more slowly than on most 60-year-olds. He carried himself with a relaxed composure that contributed to the agelessness of his appearance.

It wasn't surpising that the lovely Anita Brown has been drawn to this man over the last twenty years. She still has the firm body of a 19-year-old, and attractive abundance of curly naturally gold and brown hair, the kind that so many Californian women try to get with bleach and perms. Their son, Eli, quiet at the awkward age of 15, was a stark contrast with his rail-thin adolescent body and brown hair. Jesse, 12 (whom I met later), with lighter brown hair, was stocky and robust and more talkative. Both boys seemed younger than their ages, as did their mother and father.

The four of us went to my hotel room and I started unpacking the gifts. Everything seemed genuinely appreciated by all. As I observed during my stay, I hadn't been the butt of a joke, nor did the Siegels live in abject poverty. On an island-within-an-island off the Yucatan peninsula, they're just physically isolated from the rest of the world. English-language books are hard to get, the brown rice tastes funny (when you can get it), and for whatever reason and however ironic, Mexican beans are of poor quality. The most important parts of the isolation, however, were falling away.

JULES HAS ALWAYS BEEN INTERESTED IN TECHNOLOGY and computers, having written articles about them before the existence of the first IBM PC, and having predicted long before anyone had heard of Bill Gates that software, not hardware, would be the big money maker. He read whatever computer books and magazines he could get his hands on in Mexico, and he had a computer of his own as early as 1986, a laser printer by 1989, but he was still isolated. Jules got onto the Internet during the summer of 1996. At first, he had to visit the offices of Cancun's new Internet provider, using Faera's laptop. Before long he was tying up the phone line in the administration office of the condominium complex to dial in. In November, he got his own phone line so that he could use the Internet from his own office, and the isolation began dissolving. In many ways, this book documents his journey back into the world community as something of an adventure story.

Even for those who don't use a computer, the Internet is changing all our lives in many subtle but important ways. Those who are on the Internet are leaking new attitudes to the rest of us. Three examples:

[1] Reading and writing—literacy—is important again. The Internet is giving back what the telephone, radio and TV took away by making the written word a newly useful form of communication.

[2] Multimedia and hypertext are leaping off the computer screen and into other forms. In books, for example, new genres are pulling together subjects which used to belong on different shelves of the bookstore, and including pictures or other non-text elements in genres which were once limited to text-only.

[3] Appearances and affiliations are slowly becoming less important. On the Internet, no one knows your race or gender, the style of your clothes or the length of your hair. They know your ideas. You're free to present them to the world to stand on their own merit, whether you have any title or credentials or not.

As it turns out, Pynchon is a uniquely suitable hub for Lineland to revolve around. Not only does his work cover a fascinatingly wide range of topics, but the Internet is one of them. Jules explained to me that "*Gravity's Rainbow* is just like the Web because it begins in the middle, is told from hundreds of points of view, and everything refers to other parts of the book. It's information overload." He pointed out, "In a way, Tom saw the phenomenon of the Web and how it would change us before the technology was there. He's like William Gibson, the author of *Neuromancer*, who coined the term 'cyberspace' without even having e-mail, except that Tom was there first, much earlier."

Jules himself provides us with fascinating direct insight into the Internet as a new social and literary medium. This book is a record of conversations that took place on a mailing list—a public discussion forum in which each participant receives via e-mail a copy of every item sent to the list, and anyone can contribute comments to previous items as well as new items for discussion. You'll see many examples of the unique social interaction that takes place online in literally thousands of such forums. At the same time, you'll be struck by interesting glimpses of Jules's eventful life and his journey out of isolation; you'll enjoy the history; and, of course, you'll learn about one of our century's most literary and mysterious authors, someone who, ironically, foresaw all this.

After long absence, Jules is back. Just as he did in the 1960s and '70s, once again he is helping us to see and to define our changing world. I'm proud to have been a small part of this adventure.

—DALE L. LARSON
Publisher
INTANGIBLE ASSETS MANUFACTURING
dale@iam.com
http://www.iam.com

INTRODUCTION

My Life, Our Times

'As soon as you want something, they've got you!'
—I. F. STONE, 1907–1989

IF YOU ARE EXPECTING TO READ A BOOK ABOUT THOMAS PYNCHON, you are in the wrong place. This is a book about my experiences on the Internet, much of which takes place on an e-mail discussion list called Pynchon-L@Waste.Org. I'll tell you more about e-mail discussion lists and the Internet later on as we get into the book. In order to understand how I felt while this was all going on you will have to understand who I am and who I was. During the course of this book I will repeat this statement in one form or another, not necessarily because I tend to repeat myself (although I do) but because it is basic to what I do and who I am.

After reading this introduction, Dale L. Larson wrote me a kind of panicky e-mail letter in which he wondered if I should really begin the book with all this biography. What would some browser in Barnes & Noble make of this? Well, as I pointed out to Dale, it was the material that follows that sold him on the idea of publishing this book. We don't want to get into what his idea of a magnificent advance was because it will be a little embarrassing for everyone, especially me. Suffice it to say that I accepted it on the basis of a single phrase: **Full Creative Control**. Please note capitalization. Also note bold face emphasis. Because Dale is a man of his word and his word is his bond, the Introduction appears here just as I wrote it, except for these comments. You the reader will decide! Is Jules right? Or is Dale right? Let's take a poll!

While we are preparing the ballots here at Siegel & Children Third World Slave Labor Writing Industries, SA de CV, please read what follows carefully so that you can reply confidently when our operators call you at home or at your office to get your feedback. This could be a very important historic document, a project in which the phrase **Full Creative Control** turned out to mean **Full Creative Control**! And may God bless Dale L. Larson and all his kin down to the tenth generation and beyond for putting his blue pencil down and letting me be free to be me! In return, we'll try to exercise restraint with bold face emphasis and exclamation points from here on out.

Origins

I was born on Manhattan Island not far from Grand Central Station on October 21, 1935 at 4:05 A.M. I was a breech presentation and my mother was in labor for more than 24 hours.

I was raised mostly in The Bronx, at 1478 Walton Avenue, which was quite respectable then, but is now a burned-out skull. There were no trees on our block and few trees on all of Walton Avenue, a Berlin Wall of solid brick five- and six-story apartment houses stretching unto eternity in either direction.

My father was a petty criminal.

Although he never amounted to very much in the world, he was a good person and a good father. Everyone loved Jimmy Siegel. The character of Don Vito Corleone is based in many ways on the stories that I told Mario Puzo about my father. Mario added the grandeur and the adventure. The sadness and the dignity came from Jimmy Siegel. Who knew until *The Godfather* that criminals had families and believed in justice?

My mother was a great beauty, but like many great beauties she was vain and selfish and cruel and often insane.

My childhood

My life as a child was filled with the suffocating silence of endless fear and hidden secrets, relieved by family moments of exquisite warmth and joy, punctured by horrible disasters. My older brother tormented me viciously. When I was 25, I learned that he was my half-brother, my mother's son by a secret previous marriage. To compensate for her guilt, she favored him outrageously and treated me like the stepchild. My father, enslaved by her beauty, saw nothing. He left the house at 10 AM every weekday dressed like a banker. He came home promptly at 7 PM, a little earlier on Friday when my wailing mother lighted the *Shabbos* candles at sunset. A man of few words, what he did in between, no one knew, but I found bullets in his pockets when snitching spare change.

When I was eleven years old, my father developed viral pneumonia and had to stay home in bed for several days. He soon became delirious. He had the DTs. He was an alcoholic, although no one had ever seen him take more than a social drink. He was taken to Bronx County Hospital and was treated there for several weeks. He never drank again.

When I was twelve years old, my father disappeared for three days and we thought he had been murdered. I began to understand that life was a journey through loss. When I was fourteen, my mother had her first major episode of hysterical paranoia and was given shock treatment and hospitalized for several months. She attributed this to the stress of preparing my Bar Mitzvah celebration.

Early educational experiences

I dreaded school. In kindergarten, my first report card summed me up with "Could Do Better." I was at first unable to learn how to read or write, possibly because my eyesight was so poor, but more likely because I just wasn't ready.

I failed to grasp the simplest concepts of arithmetic. In third grade, when called to the blackboard to do sums, I had no idea what the teacher wanted. I wrote down random numbers so that she would stop bothering me.

I was diagnosed as emotionally disturbed and possibly even retarded, although my teachers did seem to suspect that I was quite intelligent.

Despite my failure to read in the true sense of the word, I was able to puzzle out the meanings of the textbooks by listening attentively in class and extrapolating skillfully from my limited understanding of the written word. I more or less faked the ability to read by memorizing the parts I couldn't get directly. I had excellent handwriting, but I was never quite clear about what I was actually writing. I also faked arithmetic in similar ways I no longer remember so clearly.

In fourth grade, I suddenly got the hang of reading and read all of the textbooks in several hours. I then had to sit through months of agonizing boredom as they went over these inane texts line by line and word by word.

My failure to concentrate was now taken as further evidence that I was mentally defective. By the age of ten I was reading dense popular novels at the rate of hundreds of words per minute. Teachers who saw me doing this accused me of faking in order to get attention. When I brought John Steinbeck's *The Red Pony* to class for a book report, the teacher urged me to find something less profound.

My friends, unlike my teachers, considered me a genius. They called me "The Brain" and "The Professor," because I had an uncanny memory and the ability to understand and explain concepts of astronomy and physics that were beyond the capacity of our parents and even our teachers.

Now that I could read, there seemed to be no limits to my ability to understand.

I found that there were many errors of fact in the textbooks, especially in science. When I gave true (as opposed to correct) answers on the examinations, I was marked wrong. When I protested and brought the references to school, they reprimanded me as a troublemaker.

In sixth grade, I achieved a score of 159 on the Stanford-Binet intelligence test. In junior high school, I scored 99% correct answers on the general reading examination, making it impossible to score the results because the system was not designed to handle that sort of performance. A couple of years later, I scored 100% correct answers on an intelligence test in a psychological clinic where I was being treated as an outpatient for playing hookey.

Instead of assuring my immediate admittance to the special rapid advance classes for gifted children, these scores fully confirmed my mental handicap and I was now ridiculed as "Mr. Potentiality."

Well, you get the picture.

A writer. An artist. The classic case.

The emerging artist

When I was ten my mother took me to Florida for the winter. A kindly teacher, very slow and southern, gave me all Es (for "excellent"—the Miami Beach equivalent of A), the first good report card of my life. She taught me how to paint. I still remember the first painting. Hibiscus. You use a thick brush to make the petals from the inside out, the color thick at the bottom, forming the trumpet. Five strokes, one for each petal. Then a thin brush for the stem and the stamens and pistils. Some yellow dots. Then a medium brush for the pointy green leaves.

She gave me an E and a compliment: "You really have remarkable artistic talent, Jules. You should pursue this."

I brought the painting to my mother. She was out on the beach behind the hotel. I handed her the painting. She handed it back without comment.

A few years later, I went to the suburban home of a rich uncle, a very modern and progressive man who had a plane, several cars, racing bicycles, skis, a typewriter and a photographic dark room. He was an exceptionally talented photographer.

He showed me how to develop pictures and to make enlargements. I then wrote 100 words about photography on the typewriter (because it was a toy) and when I came home I handed it in as my English assignment in junior high school. My English teacher, Martin Lieberman, was the faculty advisor for the *Wade News*, our school paper. He published the story.

I then went around with a girl named Enid, who had much the same characteristics that made me so popular—thick glasses, skinny, a weird family and unusual ideas—and together and separately we sold far more advertisements for the *Wade News* than it had ever had in its entire history. This earned us Silver Medals for Journalism. The Gold Medal went to a girl who wrote flowery stories that made me puke. When I got the medal, however, and the story appeared in print, my father and mother wept with joy. They bought me a camera as a reward.

So I became a writer, but all I ever really cared about was printing presses—extensions of the typewriter toy—and cameras and water color (which I soon forgot about in the face of an overwhelming family silence—they were *ashamed* of my talent). I had a phenomenal crush (mostly unrequited) on a girl named Harriet Walley (later public relations director of Sotheby's) whose older brother was studying at Visual Arts. He had some mock-ups of cigarette packages and the like. That's when I realized that an artist created them, that they were works of art. This influenced me toward what was to become a life choice—graphic design.

Professional history

After being graduated from Hunter College, I did a lot of publicity work in order to get to hang around in print shops. I became quite adept at making politicians look good in print. I worked simultaneously in the Nixon and JFK campaigns in 1960. I had a knack for making people and products famous. Eventually, I tried to give this up (because it was beneath me, you understand) and I became a free-lance writer. I have been published a lot since then. I have received some excellent reviews and personal compliments.

I hated writing. I took larger and larger doses of amphetamine and LSD to motivate myself to write. One day, in 1969, while living in Brooklyn Heights, I took a very painful dose of LSD. I was then married to Chrissie Jolly, a painter. To calm myself, I picked up her brushes and her paints and returned to kindergarten.

I remembered that I knew how to paint. More than that, I remembered that I had been forced to forget that I knew how to paint. I now began painting again regularly. I began writing out my books and manuscripts in my own handwriting. This passion continued until I lost everything I owned. I went back to writing, shall we have the cliché?—nay, the obligatory cliché?—sadder but wiser.

I am one of the few painters in the world who has ever turned to *writing* to make money. Tom Wolfe is another. I know that this will all sound like sour grapes, but eventually I had to make choices. Believe me when I tell you with no false humility that I have received some very extravagant praise for my writing. I wish I could be more appreciative of this and produce more, but I also wish that they would not ask me to write dumb things that make me want to puke.

In 1981, the Playboy Press commissioned a book to be called *The Human Robot—Essays on the Emotional Effects of Industrialism.* By now, I was married to Anita Brown, who was pregnant with Eli. Faera, my daughter with Chrissie Jolly was living with us. After Eli's birth, we all moved to Mexico on December 3, 1981. The advance on *The Human Robot* was not very large, but with some help from my mother and a loan from John Schmidt, a Colorado businessman (and *Playboy* reader) with whom Faera struck up a poolside conversation in Cabo San Lucas when she was only ten, I began putting the book together. Unfortunately, Playboy Enterprises got out of the book business before I finished. The contract was sold to Putnam, which canceled the book when I was unable to deliver it within sixty days after being notified that they were interested.

This was quite difficult to understand. Why not just wait and take a look at the manuscript? The balance of the advance was due on acceptance, so there was no risk. Laurence S. Dietz told me they had done this to every writer on the Playboy Press list and then sued them for the advances. Dietz paid. It was all economics, he thought. At the same time, how many other works like mine were aborted? How many other liberal writers tipped over the cliff into depressed silence?

I was a little sad (to say the least), but I had my publicity skills to fall back on, although, for a while, I was reduced to painting signs in Puerto Escondido, Oaxaca. In 1983, I was invited to come to Cancun to work as a publicist for FONATUR, the Mexican national tourism development fund. I have become an expert in computer graphics, as well as a publicist, and have finally achieved a life-long dream of selling my paintings. Our youngest child, Jesse, was born here in 1984. Faera also settled here and made a career for herself in eco-tourism before returning to the United States to complete her education.

I became much happier in general when I gave up writing as a way of making a living. Writing press releases is not writing in any real sense. A press release is rarely more than two pages. Two pages for a novelist is a paper napkin. Writing a book is like knitting a lawn the size of Central Park blade by blade, then clipping it into shape with nail scissors, then digging it all up and starting over again with a completely different variety of grass. When you're finished, the publisher embeds cement Frankenstein scars in the velvet smoothness with a backhoe and paints it all fluorescent green. Then he informs you that the whole thing is an unpublishable monstrosity and sues you for the advance.

I sold my typewriter and swore never to write again. Although my poverty deepened, I felt as if I had been released from the chain gang. But I missed writing, and I had to moderate the vow. I decided never again to write solely to make money, but only because I wanted to write and only what I wanted to write, as a record for my children rather than for publication. The fundamental dilemma all artists face is whether to serve Truth (with a very large capital T) or Mammon. Few publishers are willing to finance Truth, except in retrospect, when it becomes a much safer bet (and far more socially acceptable).

Publishers want the grandiose. I have no quarrel with that, but I have a little trouble providing it. I see myself as a historian, not in the sense of some Spengler or Gibbon, but in a much more primary way: a clerk keeping careful records of account on a dying planet. Some future Toynbee (who may not even be human but some highly evolved cockroach, when the meek will have inherited the earth, not to speak of the state withering away), will perhaps discover these raw materials of mine and fit them into a Big Picture. I'm more interested in the little picture. My role is merely fair witness, not to Truth, but to the truths that I saw with my own eyes and felt with my own heart. Truth is really quite humble, even a little pathetic and tattered, occasionally trying to cover some of its sadder nakednesses with little scraps of deceptive pride. Truth reveals—but also includes—deception and vanity, our failings as well as our triumphs. When I gave up writing for money, I no longer needed drugs. It's easy to write the truth. You don't have to doll it all up. You just write it.

BOQUINETE
Acrylic on paper, 24 cm. by 20 cm.
Illustration by Jules Siegel
Advertisement for Hotel Fiesta Americana Cancun, 1989

The Pursuit of Happiness

Although I never did get more than a few hot wet kisses from Harriet Walley, I have remained thin and have had the astoundingly gratifying experience of becoming better looking as I grew older. Possibly in vengeance (against Harriet, against my mother) I took unfair advantage of this for a number of years, to the detriment of my first marriages and some important friendships, but I have since reformed. I have had three wives (the latest—twenty years now—the beautiful Anita Brown, a Huguenot descendant from Wantagh, Long Island, until death do us part) many lovers and two profound affairs that scarred my heart so deeply that I vowed never to cheat again, nor to be part of any other form of triangle. I have been faithful to that vow for almost 25 years.

The rewards have been substantial. Here in the Caribbean resort of Cancun, Quintana Roo, Mexico, I accepted my fate fully. I am a formerly almost-famous writer living in a remote provincial beach city where hardly anyone speaks my language, and those who do, don't care about *The New York Times* "Best Seller" list. They do care about English language publicity, though. They do love my paintings of tropical fish and fruit and tomatoes for their menus and advertisements. I now make more money from my painting and graphic design than I do from writing, but only because I have learned to dole myself out in miserly scruples. They beg me to write. "Give us some of those *words* of yours, Don Julio," the Food and Beverage managers plead respectfully, the way I used to plead for advances from *Playboy*. I make them wait. I sell them a tomato.

When I started writing in Spanish for *Diario de Quintana Roo*, a newspaper published by the Governor's brother and some rich merchants to augment their *prestigio*, they treated me like the gringo Octavio Paz. Maybe Myron Cohen is more like it. It seems that I write with a heavy Anglo accent that sometimes makes my simplest jokes hysterically funny, my sad stories unbearably touching. They corrected my inept grammar and spelling, and wept with laughter. Cab drivers told me how wonderful I was. The newspaper paid not in cash but in copies. What did I care? I had *prestigio*.

We have awesome children. We taught Eli, now 15, and Jesse, 12, at home until they knew how to read. Now they go to a very relaxed private school—not Groton, you understand, but the kind of place adults attend to get their high school diplomas. Faera was 19 years old when she got me out of jail in exactly 45 minutes when I was falsely accused of fraud (for being much too far behind on the rent while living in an apartment hotel). It was like the New World coming to the aid of the Old. What a thrill! I felt like Maid Marian's father in *Robin Hood:* "Hit him again with the ax, Marian! I think he's still moving!" The District Attorney apologized. The lawyer refused to accept a fee. There was an investigation of the incident by the Governor's office.

"*Saludos a su papá,*" people would tell Faera warmly, "Greetings to your father." She looks like a leprechaun (the heritage of her Irish mother, the painter), but she speaks Spanish so well that people insist she's putting on airs when she tells them she was born in California. At 23 she decided to study psychoanalysis when the Puebla State College of Psychotherapists offered a course here. Now she's gone to New York and will attend New York University this Fall.

We live in a penthouse apartment we rent from fundamentally decent— indeed, saintly—landlords, James and Mae Pope, on an island within an island, overlooking the Cancun Golf Course. This is still not far enough from Walton Avenue, but how much can one person accomplish in a single lifetime? The invention of the personal computer changed my life. The arrival of the laser printer made possible a life-long dream, the ultimate extension of Uncle Irving's typewriter and darkroom and the printing press. The answer is there. How many people can actually see an answer? Freud once wrote that to become wealthy rarely produces personal happinesss because money is rarely a childhood wish. Toys are a childhood wish. To be worthy and admired is a childhood wish. I can never have my father back (he committed suicide in 1960), but I can be a good father. My mother, now gone, never became sane, but my wife is a sane and loving mother. I see before me the possibility of much happiness. I hope you do, too.

EIGHT-PAGE TABLOID NEWSPAPER SECTION

International Supplement, *Diario de Quintana Roo*, March, 1989
Text, illustration, design and typography by Jules Siegel

Created on a Panasonic Sr. Partner and a Hewlett-Packard LaserJet II
with Swfte Glyphix demo display fonts and Brøderbund's First Publisher, this was the first print project I produced on my kitchen table,
never mind the traditional start-up garage. The original wasn't as funky
as this reduced copy—all I have left for history's archives—but you'd
have to see *Diario de Quintana Roo's* production values to appreciate mine.

Part 1: Vanity

THERE'S NO BIGGER NEWS these days than the Internet, yet I sometimes wonder how many people really know what it is, especially how it started and how it works. I first heard about the Internet in 1988, at about the time I got my first very own computer, a Panasonic Sr. Partner with two 5.25-inch floppy drives and 532 kilobytes (hereinafter abbreviated as KB) of random access memory (from now on to be known as RAM). A byte consists of eight bits. Bits are the basic unit of computing, rather like the point in Euclidean geometry. Byte–bit, the cuteness never ends in programming terminology. If you think of a computer screen as highly evolved version of Etch-A-Sketch operated according to even more highly evolved principals of the same logic that Euclid used, you will know about as much as you need to know in a theoretical sense. The logic has gone a long way since Euclid, but a bit is still the exact equivalent of a point. There is really nothing about computers that Euclid would not be able to understand with a little help from Democritus, who gave us our first ideas about atoms.

Were any of these ancient Greeks to arise and be shown a computer, he would immediately stop making drawings in sand and begin using the mouse and the keyboard. And he would be smiling and laughing to himself and his wife (you can be sure that the wife or Significant Other would have arisen too) would regret ever having complained about the sand, because when night fell he used to come inside and eat. All other rivals for his affection would have eventually found others or grown old, but the computer has no rivals. It just grows more and more consuming and more and more fulfilling and once it starts talking with other computers the concept of the human family is consumed in the blinding roar of scholastic plasma.

In 1986, I had briefly rented a TRS 80, Model III, which had a then-fabulous 128 KB ram and two eight-inch floppies. Eli and I walked around it joyously singing "Com-*pu*-ter *nerds* of Mex-i-*co*!" while Jesse, then two, banged a pot with a spoon over and over again until Anita begged us to stop. If you know nothing about computing, these details will tend to make you yawn, but if your life has been changed by the personal computer the way mine was, you will smile in fond nostalgia as you recall the CPM operating system adapted by

Pickles & Trout for Radio Shack, which could manage a file containing sixteen pages of text produced in the WordStar word processing program.

The Panasonic was what was then called a "luggable," the size of a rather small suitcase, with a nine-inch composite television screen, a keyboard that also served as the lid, and an integrated thermal printer that required fax paper, which faded rapidly in the tropical humidity of Puerto Morelos, Quintana Roo, where we were then living. It came with some not very helpful manuals of Basic commands and WordStar. Other than that, I was on my own. When I turned it on and loaded its DOS 2 operating system, a little man made out of dots appeared and did a dance. Jesse still remembers him and whenever I mention the Panasonic Sr. Partner he asks me what happened to the little man.

There was only one other person who had a computer in Puerto Morelos. Although he tried to be helpful, I knew so little that he just kind of waved his hands and pointed and said, "Oh well, you'll pick it up." There were no telephones in Puerto Morelos then. I went up to Cancun and bought some computer magazines and plunged in. Not much later, after Hurricane Gilbert, we moved to Cancun and I bought a 32 megabyte (MB, from now on) hard drive and a mouse from Ing. Jorge García. The Panasonic had a non-standard serial port, so Jorge made a new interface, patiently working out the signal sequences for the mouse, which did not have any documentation.

Now that I had a mouse and a hard disk, I could run a program called First Publisher, which had been created for beginners who wanted to make greeting cards and simple menus and for sale signs. In the computer magazines, I read about a new concept called shareware, programs you could try out for the costs of the disks. Among them were typesetting fonts which could be used with First Publisher. If you liked the fonts or the progams, you sent a modest fee to the author and he or she sent you more complete versions and the manuals. I sent away for the Best Bits and Bytes shareware catalog (which had a logo of a bulldog taking a bite out of a floppy disk) and ordered a couple of dozen shareware and freeware programs. One was *The Virtual Society* by Harvey Wheeler, Martha Boaz Distinguished Research Professor at the University of Southern California. It contained the complete text of his book of the same name. From this I learned of the existence of a vast network of computers that communicated with each other along telephone lines by means of a device called a modem. "Virtual" in computer jargon means anything that exists in an electronic space bigger than the actual space defined by a given

```
   o            o            o            o            o            o           <o          <o>
 ^ | \        ^ | ^        v | ^        v | v        | / v        | X |          \ |           |
  / \          > \          / <          > \          / <          > \          / <           > \

  o>            o            o            o            o            o            o            o
   \            x          < /          < | >        < / >        < \ >        < ) >        / | \
  / <          > \          / <          > \          / <          > \          > >           / \
```

Mr. Ascii does the Macarena
Anonymous, March, 1997

Internet Humor: It's constant, hilarious and usually so intellectually advanced that it makes one feel superior while laughing. ASCII (American Standard Code for Information Exchange) is the *lingua franca* of the Internet, a set of 128 characters that any computer will read and most, if not all, will reproduce as sent. The bane of all foreign languages (because it has none of the European accented characters—which are found in the 8-bit ASCII 256 characters), it's a bit of a stiff, but in the right hands it can dance. E-mail likes ASCII and doesn't cotton to much else.

computer's active memory. Think of a window. What you can see in it is your actual space. It's surrounded by virtual space. Move the window and the virtual space becomes actual. Professor Wheeler applied this concept to the entire set of linked computers. This was the Virtual Society.

The foundation of the Virtual Society is the Internet, the world's largest computer network. The Internet grew out of research by the precursor of the Defense Department's Advanced Research Projects Agency to create a computer communication system connecting defense research centers that would remain in service even in the case of a nuclear war. This resulted in ARPANET, which went online in 1969. Over the years, more and more networks connected and it came to be known as the Internet. As of 1994, there were 30,000 computer networks connected. In 1991, then-Senator Al Gore sponsored the High-Performance Computing Act of 1991, which authorized construction of a high-speed network connecting all higher-education academic institutions, research centers, and federal organizations in the United States. This addition to the Internet is called the National Research and Education Network, and is able to transmit data at gigabit speeds (billions of bits per second.). The Internet was opened to full commercial use at the beginning of the Clinton administration.

Estimates of the number of computers connected to the Internet vary wildly, usually in the double-digit millions. One search directory, HotBot, claims to have indexed 54 million pages on the World Wide Web, probably the most popular Internet access format. A search directory is a service that helps you find something you need to know. Almost all are free, supported usually by advertising. Every time you ask HotBot a question it presents you with an ad along with the results of your query.

Because of its size, the Internet is divided into communities of interest, so many of them that many books have appeared merely cataloguing them and explaining how to use them. There are several different ways of looking at Internet information, most of which have cute names, such as Gopher and Archie and Veronica, but it appears that most users now get their access through the World Wide Web and communicate with each other by e-mail. This statement is such an over-simplification that it will undoubtedly be dismissed as mere idiocy by experienced netizens, but describing the Internet would be a life's work for all the scholars who ever were or might yet be, and I'm sure I've already told you a lot more than you want to know.

ONE OF THE FIRST THINGS I DID WHEN I GOT ONLINE a few months ago here in Cancun was to look up my own name. As Dale L. Larson has told you, I've been living in Mexico since 1981, in Cancun since 1983. I more or less stopped watching television in 1970 and I haven't seen more than a couple of dozen movies since then, most of them in the last two years. I hardly use the telephone. I've been a little out of touch. Now, of course, I am jacked in.

Much to my dismay, it turned out that as far as the Internet is concerned, I am a sub-set of the Thomas Pynchon industry, as a result of "Who Is Thomas Pynchon…and Why Is He Taking Off With My Wife?" a memoir about our friendship that I wrote for *Playboy* in 1977. Not only was the article on line, but also it turned out that it had been placed there because of interest from a group of Pynchon fans who discuss his works online. I contacted honcho Andrew Dinn to ask him about copyright notices and wound up in extensive correspondence with members of Pynchon-L@Waste.Org.

The e-mail discussion list is a truly fascinating phenomenon that evolved out of the needs of scholars to communicate with each other. There are also newsgroups that serve the similar purpose of one to many and many to one communication, but they aren't quite as easily accessible. There are some 27,000 known lists and there are people who have made careers out of simply knowing where they are. You join a list by subscribing to it. Members send their thoughts by e-mail to a central computer and all those messages go out to everyone subscribed to the list. To get off the list, you unsubscribe.

E-mail has its own culture embracing many different styles. The single most significant unifying theme is disagreement. They disagree about *everything*. Sometimes it seems all they ever do is disagree. It's like an endless ongoing debate with infinite rebuttal cycles. Some e-mail writers prefer a breezy, informal style and don't bother to check spelling or punctuation. *Playboy* Editorial Director Arthur Kretchmer: "E-mail is about speed. speed in, speed out. It's guy mail. Neatness doesn't count. If it's more than eight lines long, I don't read it." Arthur and I are having an argument about this. I think that e-mail is like any other correspondence and deserves the same respect for the reader. After I looked up my name, I looked at some sex sites and then I wrote Arthur a letter. Oh joy! To be able to communicate instantly with one of the western world's great minds and fountains of wisdom (not to speak of magazine assignments)! And not only that, to do so for free! The best thing about e-mail if you are living in Mexico is that it costs next to nothing to send an e-mail message to anyone in the world! I see we have four exclamation points in a row. A hundred would not express my enthusiasm.

To:	Arthur Kretchmer, <username@playboy.com>[1]
Subject:	Internet Virgin

We have here a new Toshiba laptop with a demonic little pointing device that sits at the intersection of the G, B & H keys. You wiggle it with the tip of your index finger, which I did so much the first few days that I injured the quick of the nail.

---

[1] Normally, we would show here an address in the form UserName@Domain.Extension. I'm sure Arthur doesn't want to get lots of email from strangers, so in order to avoid causing him any more irritation than I usually gleefully perpetrate, I am not going to put his address here.

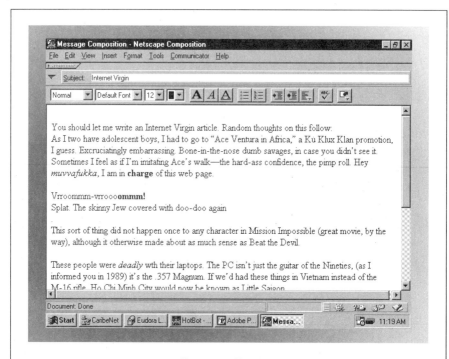

ELEGANT E-MAIL

This is how my message to Arthur looks on my screen, using the mail program that comes with Netscape Communicator, the latest version of the all-time favorite web browser that's handing Bill Gates what looks like his first major clear defeat. Unlike Eudora, which is almost but not quite straight ASCII, this program uses a language called HTML (HyperText Mark-up Language) that adds refinements such as bold, italic, even pictures, sounds and animations. It's great but it creates too many problems for people using the other mail programs, so I stick with Eudora.

The next time Anita and I made love after it healed, I used my finger with the affection more often reserved for the tongue. Afterward, she dreamily commented on how unusually *thorough* I had been. Of course—it was all that exercise on the Accupoint!

You should let me write an Internet Virgin article. Random thoughts on this follow:

As I have two adolescent boys, I had to go to "Ace Ventura in Africa," a Ku Klux Klan promotion, I guess. Excruciatingly embarrassing. Bone-in-the-nose dumb savages, in case you didn't see it. Sometimes I feel as if I'm imitating Ace's walk—the hard-ass confidence, the pimp roll. Hey *muvvafukka*, I am **in charge** of this web page.

Vrroommm-*vrroooommm!*

Splat. The skinny Jew covered with doo-doo again.

This sort of thing did not happen once to any character in "Mission Impossible" (great movie, by the way), although it otherwise made about as much sense as "Beat the Devil."

These people were *deadly* with their laptops. The PC isn't just the guitar of the Nineties, (as I informed you in 1989) it's the .357 Magnum. If we'd had these things in Vietnam instead of the M-16 rifle, Ho Chi Minh City would now be known as Little Saigon.

Computers and chicks. I have always had a thing for blondes, but you don't see Sharon Stone with a computer do you? Emanuelle Beart gave me heart palpitations. How about a nude layout of Ms. Beart jacking in to nasty sex sites. Let's *see* some of this filth corrupting the minds of our precious computer children, thereby justifying new Christian feminist anti-porn crusades. Think of the mail it will generate. What will Andrea Dworkin say about this disgusting exploitation of modern technology—after flogging herself into extreme unction with the Mixmaster vibrator attachment she's beta-testing for Martha Stewart? This is a product you definitely should cover in Potpourri. Very ecological. One motor instead of two; no landfill-contaminating batteries, either.

I haven't cheated in 25 years, but a girl who can talk about computing.... You have to think about things like that, no matter how fine sex is with the little homemaker, even if she does makes great pies, too. The premise of "Disclosure" was absolutely ridiculous. Why would anyone turn down a Demi Moore nerd? Think of the after-sex conversation!

In the course of editing all this correspondence I found it necessary to make explanatory comments that did not fit into the flow of text. To make sure that they don't get confusing, I've set them in a distinctive style, as here. Attached to this message to Arthur was a photograph of a very beautiful blonde girl in a lusciously elegant and tasteful setting inserting a large black dildo into the rectum of another young woman whose exceptionally well-formed buttocks filled the lower third of the frame. This was the "Picture of the Week" from SuckSex.Com, one of the Web's more imaginative sex sites. The photograph was in a format known as JPEG, for the Joint Photographic Experts Group, which after years of arduous negotiation agreed on a standard for compressing photographs with a minimum loss of detail so that they can be transmitted more rapidly over the Internet. Confident that the combination of text and picture would result in an immediate assignment, I eagerly awaited Arthur's reply to my enthusiastic idea.

From: Arthur Kretchmer
Subject: Your last message

Jules,

Your e-mail logs in with the rest of the e-mail and then I pretty much don't read it.

Unfortunately, your e-mail has a habit of locking up my office Mac. So not only do you tell me more than I ever want to know, you also prevent other people from communicating with me until your messages are cleared from the server. It happens frequently enough that I'm going to have your messages kept out of the system.

I've asked the system operator to explain why jpegs from David Sheff and Bruce Kluger get through, but yours bring the system to its knees.

—AK

Well. Things don't always work out the way you think they should. This often results not only in lock-ups and system crashes, but also in torrents of strange characters called "garbage" pouring across your screen. In editing this book, I've moved things around freely and organized the many different styles into what I feel is a more coherent text stream, as I don't think that raw e-mail lends itself to the kind of extended reading a book invites. Like regular letters, e-mail messages don't always arrive in the exact sequence they were sent. Other messages intervene. Sometimes answers from others come to a message that hasn't yet arrived on your desktop. A reply to a message includes snippets of the original to pin down the specific point being addressed.

Threads are loosely joined by subject lines, which often fray and separate on tangential discussions. This is often fascinating online, but results in too much text to follow very well in a book. You have here, then, not a transcript of e-mail conversation, but an interpretation. If you would like to see what the public side of this conversation looked like online, fire up your computer and your Web browser and go to:

```
http://www.cee.hw.ac.uk/~andrew/pynchon-l.html
```

This address is known as a URL, for "Universal Resource Locator." From Andrew's website, follow the instructions to the Pynchon-L Archive and then do a search for October and November, 1996. There you will find the original unedited sources of this book. I look forward to seeing your scholarly exegesis on this: "From Bytes to Type: Transmutations of Meaning in the Pynchon-L–to–*Lineland* Datastream." Meanwhile, let us begin our epic *in media res*. Andrew is responding to a previous letter. In good Internet style, he's quoting the relevant snippets from my previous letter to him.

From:	andrew@cee.hw.ac.uk (Andrew Dinn)
To:	Jules Siegel <jsiegel@mail.caribe.net.mx>
Subject:	*Re:* More on Pynchon article

YOU WROTE: *It occurred to me that the way around the problem is for me to put the article online. It was a really good piece that I enjoyed writing and it created quite a sensation when it came out. You could then reference the URL for your friends and other interested parties. This will be good public relations and good commerce. I still have to work for a living and I need the publicity.*

ANDREW: O.K., I am quite happy to arrange things this way around. Do you want an electronic copy marked up for the web or do you already have one? If the former then I can probably retrieve a version of my old web page from the backup tapes—assuming the computing officers have not screwed up, that is.

JULES: We are quite commercial here at Siegel World Writing Industries. Pynchon made quite a thing of being mysterious. I am just a vulgar Jew from the Bronx. I once wrote an article for *Penthouse* and Gay Bryant, a veddy British lady editor, called to tell me that they wanted certain absurd changes. I referred to the divine right of artistic integrity.

"There is no question of artistic integrity," she replied crisply, sounding rather like Margaret Thatcher on a bad day. "This is a commercial enterprise devoted to making the owners rich. You'll make the changes or you won't get paid."

"I've already been paid," I answered and hung up on her. They published the piece as I wrote it. The moral of this story is that it always best to get paid in advance. And never to forget those immortal words: "This is a commercial enterprise devoted to making the owners rich."

ANDREW: Artistic integrity is not really a major concern in the software business. It's not that we have no desire to produce world-beating, ground-breaking programs—the Great American Compiler or some such. But the engineering process is pretty rigid and limited in its outlook. It rapidly gets drilled into your head that you are a drone there to build some other sucker's design, usually for an accounting package. All the real software playboys are to be found in small start-ups. Or, like me, they have retired to University where they can pretend they are designing the next generation's answers to the last generation's problems while in reality they are mostly just exercising the capabilities of their esteemed institution's high-speed Internet links. But I'll remember the tip about being paid in advance should I ever take up consulting again.

From: andrew@cee.hw.ac.uk (Andrew Dinn)
Subject: *Re:* More on Pynchon article II

JULES SIEGEL *writes*: I have the piece. I retrieved it from my cache when you said you had deleted it. I made some corrections—typos. I will put it online tonight, but it may take a couple of days to be available, as the webmaster here does everything himself. I'll send you the URL etc. when I know it's on. Meanwhile, send me yours as I didn't bookmark it and I erase everything as soon as I'm finished.

ANDREW: My URL for the article? Or for my pages? The article is no longer there but my web pages are accessible via:

```
http://www.cee.hw.ac.uk/~andrew/
```

The Pynchon archive and all the other Pynchon related pages are accessible from:

ANDREW DINN'S WEB PAGE

Here you see Andrew's Web page, which with true British reserve, is quite austere. You are looking at it through a browser, in this case Netscape Communicator 2.0. Netscape grew out of a University of Illinois browser called Mosaic, which is still around but struggling a bit for air. Some graduate students who worked on Mosaic went off and formed their own company and got some venture capitalists to back them. Released from the stuffy constraints of academe, they came up with a high-energy browser that made everything else look decidedly lame and now they are all billionaires. The kids who stayed behind sound quite jealous when they tell their side of the story. Nonetheless, Bill Gates *fears* these teenagers at Netscape even though they aren't really teenagers anymore but just look that way by comparison. They are young but they are sharp. Microsoft Internet Explorer is struggling with security bugs that make all computers using it more or less open books to hackers. He claims that this is fixed. Some don't agree. Netscape, supposedly, has no such bugs. *Uh-*oh.

```
http: //www.cee.hw.ac.uk/~andrew/pynchon-1.html
```
(that's pynchon with a dash ell, not pynchon with a dash one).

The reference to your article was in amongst all the other journalism on page:

```
http: //www.cee.hw.ac.uk/~andrew/pynchon-misc.html
```

I will install your url when you have prepared your version of the article. At the moment the link for the *Playboy* article points at:

```
http: //www.cee.hw.ac.uk/~andrew/siegel.html
```

This latter page contains a recommendation to mail you or apply to *Playboy* for a copy.

JULES: I joined the Pynchon list. I never knew he aroused such Talmudic discussion. I liked *V.*, but the rest of his work left me cold.

ANDREW: You should browse the archives. We've covered just about everything in the last 4-5 years. But Talmudic? Not sure exactly what you mean by that—literally Talmudic or in the style of? Are you a practicing Jew? I know something of the religion but not enough to penetrate the mysteries of *Habbakuk, Sepharoth* etc. which Pynchon sneaks into *Gravity's Rainbow*.

JULES: I am an unpractising Jew. Nothing like eating pork in Mexico on *Yom Kippur* (the Day of Atonement—vigilant fasting and life revision as if facing the Last Judgment). The *Talmud* is essentially an extended argument about law, culture and custom, rather like the *Variorum Edition* of Shakespeare. It was the first hypertext document, but you have to see it in Hebrew to understand why. Dense textual analysis to the max, with footnotes on footnotes.

ANDREW: Judging by comments on the list a lot of those who read *V.* first (particularly early after it arrived) find it hard to get into the rest of his work, especially *Gravity's Rainbow*. How many times did you try reading it? Most people, even the fanatics, give up on it at least once. I liked *V.*, in particular the scenes in South Africa. But *Gravity's Rainbow* is so vast and all-encompassing I have not read anything to compare with it—maybe Joyce or William Gaddis (or even Melville) gets nearest. Also, the style and structure are incredibly inventive and yet it's easily readable, unlike say Gaddis who requires vast amounts of concentration.

JULES: *Gravity's Rainbow* was mildly interesting. I wonder if anyone has commented on what it means: we are *Gravity's Rainbow*. You know—the spectrum is a manifestation of light energy. So *Gravity's Rainbow* would be the spectrum of gravity—all that has mass, I guess. But I don't really think it applies, because gravity isn't energy; it's an effect of the shape of space, supposedly. I think it's really just another manifestation of what we call sexual attraction, love, that which brings one to join with another.

ANDREW: Bravo Jules, but you should be writing this to the list. Others have played with that idea but usually without communicating what lies behind it so succinctly and cogently.

JULES: What I did like about *Gravity's Rainbow* is the way it demythologized military service. It was the view from the tin can, the destroyer, the minesweeper—scummy and snotty and dirty and wet and totally lacking in romance.

ANDREW: Yeah but then again what about *The Naked and the Dead*? Didn't that do the same job? (at least the opening 100 pages—much of the rest is unnecessary). Or is there still too much macho stuff in that book?

JULES: I found most of Pynchon's science rather shallow, although he did get the feeling of scientists. He got SHOCK and SHROUD from a brochure I gave him. He had a great capacity for synthesizing things in a way that looks like profound research, but is really a similar kind of pastiche.

ANDREW: Well, it seems that not many people can see the joins unless they are pointed out. But you are right that his skill is synthesis, not analysis. And if it is only a matter of feeling then I am even more impressed because I know a fair bit of science and I rarely find that he has put a foot wrong. I cannot believe that he is not *au fait* with the relevant first principles as well as the mood.

Hope you enjoy sitting in on the list or maybe even contributing a few notes.

Cheers,

—Andrew Dinn
And though Earthliness forget you,
To the stilled Earth say: I flow.
To the rushing water speak: I am.

Most mail programs allow you automatically to append a standard signature to your messages. Sometimes these include little pictures constructed with standard typewriter characters. On Pynchon-L, we see literary quotations such as Andrews' from Rilke. Every time Andrew posts a message to the list it ends with these lines. We'll just use signatures once and you can fill in the rest. Not all the postings to a list are directly on-topic. Sometimes they tend to wander so far off-topic that users begin complaining and the list owner has to assert control. Pynchon-L is quite disorderly in this respect, rather like an animated literary cocktail party burbling along on a stream of consciousness more or less contained by the group reading of Gravity's Rainbow *which we will encounter a little further along. People often post things that have nothing to do with Thomas Pynchon but might have some filial relationship with his brand of humor, as in the following item on the Ig Nobel Awards. Sometimes they get into wild arguments along tangents that might be more appropriate in some political caucus, just as they would at a real literary cocktail party. If you keep that metaphor in mind, you will have no problems with the list's meandering flow of electronic conversation.*

From:	Wolfe, Skip <crw4@nip1.em.cdc.gov>
To:	Pynchon-L <pynchon-l@waste.org>
Subject:	Ig Nobel Prizes

I thought those interested in taking a brief break from *Gravity's Rainbow* might enjoy the following summary.

Here are the winners of the 1996 Ig Nobel Prizes, presented at the Sixth First Annual Ig Nobel Prize Ceremony, held at Sanders Theater, Harvard University on Thursday evening, October 3, 1996. The Prizes were handed out by genuine Nobel Laureates Dudley Herschbach, William Lipscomb, and others.

The Prizes honor people whose achievements "cannot or should not be reproduced."

This year's ceremony featured the world premiere of "Lament Del Cockroach," a mini-opera starring mezzo-sopranos Margot McLaughlin and scientist/Supermodel Symmetra as cockroaches and the Nobel Laureates as insects eager to mate. At the opera's conclusion, a meteorite from Mars eradicated the roaches while three plants sang Handel's Hallelujah Chorus ("Hallelujah! Hallelujah! Hallelujah! The roaches are gone!") and Earth's other life forms danced the macarena.

BIOLOGY: Anders Baerheim and Hogne Sandvik of the University of Bergen, Norway, for their tasty and tasteful report, "Effect of Ale, Garlic, and Soured Cream on the Appetite of Leeches." [The report was published in "British Medical Journal," vol. 309, Dec. 24-31, 1994, p. 1689.] Drs. Baerheim and Sandvik sent a videotaped acceptance speech, and watched the ceremony live on the Internet.

MEDICINE: James Johnston of R.J. Reynolds, Joseph Taddeo of U.S. Tobacco, Andrew Tisch of Lorillard, William Campbell of Philip Morris, and the late Thomas E. Sandefur, Jr., chairman of Brown and Williamson Tobacco Co. for their unshakable discovery, as testified before the US Congress, that nicotine is not addictive.

PHYSICS: Robert Matthews of Aston University, England, for his studies of Murphy's Law, and especially for demonstrating that toast always falls on the buttered side. [The report, "Tumbling toast, Murphy's Law and the fundamental constants" was published in "European Journal of Physics," vol. 16, no. 4, July 18, 1995, p. 172-6.] Professor Matthews sent an audiotaped acceptance speech.

PEACE: Jacques Chirac, President of France, for commemorating the fiftieth anniversary of Hiroshima with atomic bomb tests in the Pacific.

PUBLIC HEALTH: Ellen Kleist of Nuuk, Greenland and Harald Moi of Oslo, Norway, for their cautionary medical report "Transmission of Gonorrhea Through an Inflatable Doll." [The report was published in "Genitourinary Medicine," vol. 69, no. 4, Aug. 1993, p. 322.] Dr. Moi traveled from Oslo to Cambridge—at his own expense—to accept the Prize. During the trip, Dr. Moi also delivered a lecture at Harvard Medical School about his achievement.

CHEMISTRY: George Goble of Purdue University, for his blistering, world record time for igniting a barbecue grill—three seconds, using charcoal and liquid oxygen. Professor Goble's colleague Joe Cychosz traveled to Cambridge to accept the Prize.

BIODIVERSITY: Chonosuke Okamura of the Okamura Fossil Laboratory in Nagoya, Japan, for discovering the fossils of dinosaurs, horses, dragons, princesses, and more than 1000 other extinct "mini-species," each of which is less

---

CALL FOR PAPERS, PLEASE POST

Languaging: The Ninth Annual Conference on Linguistics and Literature.

Sponsored by the Department of English and the Graduate Students in English at the University of North Texas, 7-8 February 1997, Radisson Hotel and Conference Center, Denton, Texas

KEYNOTE SPEAKERS: **Mark Turner,** University of Maryland. Author of *Death is the Mother of Beauty* (1987), *Reading Minds* (1991), and *The Literary Mind* (forthcoming). **George Lakoff,** University of California, Berkeley Author of *Metaphors We Live By* (with Mark Johnson, 1980), *Women, Fire and Dangerous Things* (1987), and *Moral Politics* (1996).

SPECIAL FEATURE: "Languaging" with Lakoff and Turner, co-authors of *More than Cool Reason* (1989). Collaborative Address. Luncheon hosted by Haj Ross.

ALTHOUGH we especially encourage submissions dealing with cogni - tive linguistics, conceptual metaphor, and linguistic analysis of literature, we welcome abstracts dealing with any aspect of linguistics or literature, including: Literary Analysis, Linguistic Analysis, Composition Theory, ESL/EFL, Critical Theory, Theoretical Linguistics, Composition/ESL, Pedagogy, 1st/2nd Language Acquisition Minority Literature, Women's Studies, Film Theory/Popular Culture, Creative Writing.

DEADLINE FOR SUBMISSIONS: 15 October 1996 Notified by: 30 November 1996. Conference proceedings will be published. Creative submissions of poetry, fiction or essays are also welcome, as are proposals for complete symposia. For more information, please contact: Languaging: the Ninth Annual Conference on Linguistics and Literature University of North Texas Department of English P. O. Box 13827 Denton, TX 76203 *E-mail:* linglit@unt.edu *Fax:* 817/565-4355

ELECTRONIC BULLETIN BOARD ANNOUNCEMENT

Think of the e-mail literary cocktail party as taking place in the Faculty Lounge. Here's one of the kind of things you'll see posted.

than 1/100 of an inch in length. [For details see the series "Reports of the Okamura Fossil Laboratory," published by the Okamura Fossil Laboratory in Nagoya, Japan during the 1970s and 1980s.]

LITERATURE: The editors of the journal *Social Text*, for eagerly publishing research that they could not understand, that the author said was meaningless, and which claimed that reality does not exist.

[The paper was "Transgressing the Boundaries: Toward a Transformative Hermeneutics of Quantum Gravity," Alan Sokal, *Social Text*, Spring/Summer 1996, pp. 217-252.]

ECONOMICS: Dr. Robert J. Genco of the University of Buffalo for his discovery that "financial strain is a risk indicator for destructive periodontal disease."

ART: Don Featherstone of Fitchburg, Massachusetts, for his ornamentally evolutionary invention, the plastic pink flamingo. Mr. Featherstone traveled to Cambridge to accept the Prize.

The ceremony also included an auction of plaster casts of the left feet of four Nobel Laureates, and several tributes to the concept of "Biodiversity." Thirteen-year old Kate Eppers, spokesperson for the Committee for Bacterial Rights, said:

"We live in a diverse society. Our biggest ethnic groups are not the Asians, the Africans or the Caucasians. Our biggest ethnic groups are the Bacteria. I used to wash my hands every day. My mom made me. But then I learned about ethnic cleansing. Every time you wash your hands, you wipe out billions and billions of Bacteria. That's not fair. Bacteria have rights, too. So let's be grown-ups about this. When mom asks you to wash your hands, just say No."

Further details—including shocking photos—will be posted in our web site (http://www.improb.com) during the coming months.

From: rr.tfcny@mail.fdncenter.org
Subject: Smoking Banana Peels

Leafing through my recently purchased *Mad* about the Sixties came across a Don Martin cartoon which depicts this groovy dude chopping up some 'nanas peel, ground to fine powder, then stuffing into a little pipe, smoking, with no effect, gets mad, eyebrows all akinder that Don Martin way, takes a step, slips on the leftover 'nana peel, hits the back of his head on the counter, begins to see groovy things about the air, including stars, wavy clouds, and other fine points of trippiness flight...the myth continues, now about that nutmeg...

—Richard Romeo
Coordinator of Cooperating Collections
The Foundation Center-NYC

David Nevin Friedman <namdeirf@gwis2.circ.gwu.edu> wrote:

Anyone desperate enough to smoke banana peels is pretty pathetic...but then again, this mailing list is about Thomas Pynchon and his characters whose psychoses make us look rational...smoke on!

J.D._P._Lafrance@ridley.on.ca wrote:

Interestingly enough, a folk-punk band, The Dead Milkmen did a song called "Smokin' Banana Peels" in the mid-'80s! very trippy, mondo-bizarro vibe on that song too...

From: georgej@georgejames.com
Subject: Etienne Cherdlu

In TP's short story there is a character called Etienne Cherdlu (a fat boy keen on practical jokes).

Referring to this character in a recent conversation someone noticed that Etienne Cherdlu was rather similar to ETAOIN SHRDLU.

What is ETAOIN SHRDLU I hear you ask? Here is the explanation that he gave:

"The Linotype keyboard was arranged approximately in order of English letter frequency, E being most common, T next common, and so on. When an operator was aware of a typographical error, the line needed to be filled out to allow the slug to be completed. This was done by running hands along the keyboard, so the slug would typically say something like "typographical error etaoin shrdlu..." Of course, the kind of Linotype machines I'm talking about haven't been used since the seventies... the ones originally invented by Merganthaler, which made a lot of noise and literally cast slugs in hot lead."

Can anyone confirm the origin of this name? Does anyone know anything more about Linotype keyboards? Did TP ever use or encounter one? What about the names of other characters in his books?
—George James

From: pelovitd@gusun.acc.georgetown.edu
Subject: *Re:* Smoking Banana Peels

It was my understanding that the "smoking bananas" craze in the Sixties started from the Donovan song "Mellow Yellow." Interesting that Pynchon has illustrated almost every form of drug use/abuse except this one.
—David L. Pelovitz, Ph.D.

From: tstanton@nationalgeographic.com
Subject: *Re:* Etienne Cherdlu

Did TP ever use or encounter one?

Linotypes were common in the Sixties, so TP could easily have encountered one on a tour of a newspaper in HS or college. My guess is this obscure fact is documented somewhere & was filed away until it could be used. Wonder if there's a character named "*Lorem Ipsum*" anywhere. These are the first 2 words in a Latin text that is commonly used to "Greek" a type layout.
—Tom Stanton

From: Jules Siegel <jsiegel@pdc.caribe.net.mx>
Subject: Banana peels

The banana peel smoking fad of the Summer of Love, 1967, was probably started as a hoax. It somehow became public belief that the dried inside of the banana peel was high in serotonin and would get you high. I remember a parade of banana peel supporters in the East Village, carrying the appropriate banners and wearing banana costumes (very revealing, you can be sure). This was one of the high points of the Summer of Love, itself probably the high point of the psychedelic revolution.

---

grip@netcom.com wrote:

There is a chapter in Hofstadter's *Goedel, Escher, Bach: an Eternal Golden Braid*, titled "SHRDLU, Toy of Man's Designing" which consists of a dialog between a human, Eta Oin, and a computer program, SHRDLU.

Later, in the next chapter—Hofstadter likes to keep explanations at bay, and reveal them only later after the reader has had lots of time to puzzle over their meaning—he explains that ETAOIN SHRDLU was "…used by Linotype operators to mark typos in newspaper columns." He doesn't explain just how these are used. I deduced, correctly I believe, that the letters are in the same order as their frequency of appearance in standard English language texts. It seems to me that there has been some small shift in this arrangement in the last few years, but generally it is true.

If you haven't read Hofstadter's first work, try it. It is a delightful book, although tough sledding in some of the more technical aspects such as Goedel's incompleteness theorem.

—grip

David Caesuras <casseres@apple.com> wrote:

I wouldn't read too much into Pynchon's use of a play on the string ETAOIN SHRDLU. It's a very familiar thing to people older than, say, 50. Many of us used it for years to stand for "a meaningless string of letters" without being aware of its origins in the top row of keys on a Linotype. Pynchon makes names out of all sorts of bits and pieces of common usage, often without much effort to exploit the original meanings.

Cheers,

—David

The following message is typical of the responses to the **Gravity's Rainbow** *Group Reading. Andrew Dinn previously posted a set of questions about a specific section of the text and Chris Karatnytsky has responded. I am not going to reproduce much more than this sample because most of it is heavy going unless you are participating in the project. The entire group reading, which has been in process for four years, can be inspected in the Pynchon-L Archive, which is by far the most useful tool for understanding* **Thomas**

Pynchon's writing. Chris's message appears pretty much as it came across my screen, but I've converted her e-mail *emphasis* and _citation_ conventions to typographical style.

From:	ckaratnytsky@nypl.org
Subject:	GRGR2

Re question 1: Well, Skippy, the computer's been crashing and the network's up and down, but I've got some thoughts, specifically in re the introduction of Slothrop, which run as follows: I agree with Andrew's comment that P's attention to detail is awesome (in this word's literal, as well as it's, um, pothead usage—totally) in this section, but I don't entirely agree that it's disparate. Moreover, though I don't *disagree* that the "stage directions and scenery …introduce but…don't explore in detail later obsessions," I would like to say that, well, yes, this may be true, but I think that the comment is off the point a bit: I think that the stage directions and scenery explore PREVIOUS obsessions, namely, The Dream, and certain images and associations that were put into place in section 1.

Things that link:

Think about Slothrop's extreme discomfort at the sound of the rockets. "But then last September the rockets came. Them fucking rockets. *You couldn't adjust to the bastards.*" [Emphasis added.] A-and—remember Slothrop's increasing distress as the bombings get worse—the chain-smoking, the nervousness, the drinking, etc. (Tantivy kids him about smoking two cigs at once…)

Now compare all of this with the introductory Dream graph ("A screaming comes across the sky. *It has happened before, but there is nothing to compare it to now.*" [Emphasis added.]) and the intense fatalism and grim claustrophobia of the evacuation. This sense of continued, relentless torment in the face of repeated bombings mirrors Slothrop's terror to such an extent that it makes for a pretty strong connection in my (pot)head, anyway. I think that we're being shown that Surrogate Dreamer Prentice has been having Slothrop's dream.

Yes I do, Skippy.

Also (big also): I think the use of italics in the Dream section in the Slothrop/current reading section, esp. after young Tyrone has a freak out while watching the Northern Lights display, merits closer attention. That Voice, those italics, is an echo from section 1. A-and: "It was one of those great iron afternoons in London..." Iron, anyone? 'Nother echo.

Re question 7: The map is another link to the Dream, if I'm understanding it correctly. A star for every girl that Tyrone's boinked, right? And the stars and the girls and the boinks correspond to the bombings, right? Well, then, if so, remember this from section 1: The "ruinous secret cities of poor, *places whose names he has never heard...*" [Emphasis P.] If the "he" here is not Prentice (couldn't be, right?) but Tyrone, then the line is a ref to those site visits he's been making. How about that, Skippy?

Re question 10: The Hooker quote and the description of "how Slothrop's garden grows" (page 22 in the paperback) recalls the Chap. 1 observation "this is not a disentanglement from, but a progressive knotting into" and builds on other images of waste and entropy, growth and decay... Think "love-in-idleness." The Dickinson quote ("Ruin is formal, devil's work..) and the Constant Slothrop verse, with its varied images of "knotting into" ("Loom of God" and "threads of His Love") build on these same images...

Comments?

—Chris

To: ckaratnytsky@nypl.org
From: Jules Siegel <jsiegel@caribe.net.mx>
Subject: GRGR2 :

I just love this. This is so dense, my head is spinning. What you need is to have Tom here to read the text in question out loud, using funny voices appropriate to each speaker. Now just do it yourself: the Voice of God, a terrified news announcer, Hal the Robot... like that.

About his method (Manhattan Beach, 1966):

"I'm walking along a street with a long, high, bright green wood plank fence that stretches blocks in either direction. A red door opens in it and a security guard in blue police uniform steps out carrying a bouquet of roses. That's what I write about."

He takes scenes like this and places them in a framework that he sees, but you don't, like an invisible crossword puzzle. I would advise you to look for a structure such as the periodic table of the elements. Start by counting the number of chapters. Then see if there is a well-known table of constants that fits it. Each chapter will then be an iconic illustration (i.e. Eros with bow and arrow and blindfold—love is blind) of the state of energy expressed by that number in the table.

---

ckaratnytsky@nypl.org wrote:

Many thanks for your kind words, but, lissen—thought you'd want to know that you posted to me only and not the p-list. I think the quote you cited and your comments bear repeating for the benefit of all. O.K. if I forward? Or—do you wanna do it?

Chris, I was a little concerned about your reaction (I meant dense in the sense of close textual analysis) and grateful to receive your note. Actually, I didn't know that it hadn't been posted, but I'm kind of glad it wasn't. I joined the list as a result of finding Andrew Dinn's copy of my article on Pynchon. I'm usually quite impulsive about shooting my mouth off, but, as I told Andrew, I feel I want to be a bit more formal here.

I am probably going to write an introductory essay first and see his response to my observations before circulating it generally. Since you've proved to be non-paranoid psychotic as well, I'll copy it to you. I read *V.* when it first came out. I only skimmed *Gravity's Rainbow*—mostly I'm sure, because I was still quite hurt and resentful, so I didn't really give it a fair chance. It's very hard for me to get interesting books here. If someone has a spare copy of *Gravity's Rainbow* it would be extremely helpful for me to have it. Express Mail ($10.50) from US gets here in four to five days.

We (Anita, my beautiful wife, and our heroically handsome children, Eli, 15, and Jesse, 12) are starved for stimulating books in English. Anyone who sends us books will receive a handsomely printed "Award of Merit for Service to Humanity" endorsed with his/hers/its name in type. Suitable for framing, one can use this to refute charges of social uselessness.

> *I later posted the previous two messages to Chris Karatnytsky to the entire list, along with some others I had inadvertently sent as private e-mail. Here is Chris's response to my message. Quotes are usually indicated by a > symbol at the beginning of the line. Some browsers translate this into italic, as I've done here. I don't do this in a very consistent manner, usually just for short "he said–she said" ex-*

'I wasn't psychotic the last time I checked.'

changes. Where the quotations are longer and attributions are more complicated, I use the *"*JULES*:–*ANDREW*:" format.*

From:	ckaratnytsky@nypl.org
Subject:	oh *sure* you did
To:	Jules Siegel <jsiegel@mail.caribe.net.mx>

YOU WROTE: *(I meant dense in the sense of close textual analysis)*

Hehhehheh. I wuz thinking about making a joke to the effect ("Dense, Mr. Seigel? Hmmm…[Insert joke here.]"), but, as I had never seen you post b4, I, usually quite impulsive about shooting my mouth off (hey, where've I heard that before?), thought I should refrain from smartass humor. Nice to meetcha. I *thought* it was you, as in, I read your piece, yes, through Andrew's good graces, and remembered your name.

I am probably going to write an introductory essay first and see his response to my observations before circulating it generally. Since you've proved to be non-paranoid psychotic as well, I'll copy it to you.

I'd like to read it. Thanks. (Caveat: I wasn't psychotic the last time I checked, but, oh, I don't know about that non-paranoid part there. This list (quite unlike some others I'm on) weirds me out sometimes. Feeds my normal level of paranoia like you wouldn't be–LIEVE, but that's the territory, I guess. I'm currently working on the theory that I'm the only *real* participant and that everybody else's responses are being written by the same (other) person with a gazillion e-mail accounts. Major conspiracy going on here. Whoa…)

I read V. *when it first came out. I only skimmed* Gravity's Rainbow—*mostly I'm sure, because I was still quite hurt and resentful, so I didn't really give it a fair chance.*

I recently finished GR for the first time a coupla weeks ago, after nearly 10 failed years trying. Quite the trip. Nothing like it. I empathize with your feelings. If such things matter in the face of personal pain, your Pynchon piece was an eloquent memoir of that time.

It's very hard for me to get interesting books here.

Well that's something we can work on. What are you doing down there, anyway? Never been to Mexico. Have wanted to go for a long time.

If someone has a spare copy of Gravity's Rainbow *it would be extremely helpful for me to have it. Express Mail ($10.50) from US gets here in four to five days.*

I don't have a spare, but I'd be happy to pick one up somewhere for you. Or, anything else that you or the family care to put in a request for... Let me know.
        Best wishes to all.
                —Chris

P.S. B-but are you *sure* you don't want everyone to know how smart, uh, uh, I mean, dense I am?

From:	Brett Coley <bcoley@vnet.ibm.com>
To:	pynchon-l@waste.org
Subject:	*Re:* pronounciation

PAUL DIFILIPPO flipped his lid and said: *Watching the Clinton-Dole debate last night, was I the only person to distinctly hear our Prez talk about insuring that all Americans had access to some kind of "Pynchon plan"? I'm not sure, but I think it has something to do with all of us reading* Gravity's Rainbow *after we retire!!!*

And CRAIG CLARK added: *I'm afraid you're mistaken, Paul. The original plan was supply every American household with access to free Pynchon texts, but then the Republicans objected and said that TRP was too "un-American" (a sop to the wing of the party which supported Buchanan), so Slick Willy Clinton struck a compromise deal to ensure that all Americans have access to some kind of "Pyncheon Plan", i.e. an abridged version of Hawthorne's "House of the Seven Gables".*

I just picture thousands of senior citizens wearing godzilla shirts and baggy pants roaming the streets of the nation's major cities casting suspicious glances over their shoulders, occasionally breaking into bawdy song and a spontaneous two-step ...
        Wow, that is a true "Vision for America".

I can see it. Maybe Clinton could too, after all, how could you not inhale? Seriously now. What about that Bob Dole? Do you think he might be O.K. if he drank about a fifth of scotch? He almost got a little surreal during the debates the other night, he would be answering some question, then he would wander off on some comment about the President signing some bill after midnight or something, but then he would remember where he was and get back on the script... I kept flashing to Major Pudding for some reason when that would happen, all that WWII flashback stuff Bob Dole was doing, I suppose.

Bill, of course, never departed from the script. Sorry for the political digression. We now return you to your regularly scheduled e-mail.

Jules Siegel <jsiegel@pdc.caribe.net.mx> wrote:

A government agent on duty would take the joint to avoid calling attention to himself, but he would not inhale because he would not want to lose control.

From:	Dkipen@aol.com
To:	jsiegel@pdc.caribe.net.mx
Subject:	You're alive!

Dear Mr. Siegel,

I'm assuming I can't be the only Pynchon-lister who recognized your name. Are they all e-mailing you under separate cover in hopes of private lore nuggets to call their own? Or am I just being, er, paranoid? Anyway, glad to hear of your continuing respiration. I work at *Daily Variety,* whose Mexico correspondent Andrew Paxman once told me of a delightful evening you two spent at an early installment of the now, alas, apparently dormant Cancun Film Festival. What are you up to these days? Ever get back to LA? What prompted you to visit the p-list, or have you been lurking all this time, biting your lip even during occasional flattering references re your own contributions to the literature?

Best,

—David Kipen

From:	Jules Siegel <jsiegel@mail.caribe.net.mx>
To:	Dkipen@aol.com
Subject:	*Re:* You're alive!

Dkipen@aol.com wrote:

Dear Mr. Siegel,

Jules, please. When people call me Mr. Siegel, I look around for my father.

I'm assuming I can't be the only Pynchon-lister who recognized your name.

One of the first.

What are you up to these days?

Sitting up and taking a little nourishment. For more, see my website, referenced below.

Ever get back to LA?

Haven't been in the US since Dec. 3, 1981.

What prompted you to visit the p-list?

Vanity. The first thing I did when I got online was to look for my own name. Seems I'm mostly a subset of the Pynchon industry.

Nice hearing from you, David. Say hi to Andrew and tell him I'm sorry I couldn't deliver the Cancun story for him when he was at *Excelsior.*

From:	Dkipen@aol.com
To:	jsiegel@pdc.caribe.net.mx
Subject:	*Re:* You're alive!

Dear Jules,

I'm sorry you haven't been well. Not that hip acting up again, I hope.

So how does the Pynchon-list look to someone with your privileged perspective? Does it strike you as a whole lotta hullabaloo to devote to someone you've probably thrown pillows at for snoring? By the way, I'd be unworthy of even my small place in the Pynchon industry if I didn't ask whether you ever heard tell of any reaction on his part to "Who the Hell Is Thomas Pynchon…?" (Your title, I'm wondering?) This is what you get for vanity. When I type my name into most search engines, I get either an offer to buy my own book, *The Film Producers, Studios, Agents and Casting Directors Guide*—a steal at $45—or "Sorry, no items returned for 'David Kipen.'"

To: Dkipen@aol.com
Subject: Your questions

DKIPEN@AOL.COM WROTE: *I'm sorry you haven't been well. Not that hip acting up again, I hope.*

Yes. I don't remember complaining, though, as I usually try to keep these things to myself.

So how does the Pynchon-list look to someone with your privileged perspective? Does it strike you as a whole lotta hullabaloo to devote to someone you've probably thrown pillows at for snoring?

It's fun. I liked *V.*—after certain reservations (and their amusing resolution), which I will discuss later online for all—but the rest of his work was not my cup of tea. I am, perhaps, obsessively devoted to clarity and accessibility, not only as a writer, but also as a graphic designer. I am also unimpressed by much of what passes as "academic" literature and "fine" art. I think performance art and installation art are mostly doper hoaxes. I'm into hyper-realism and traditional typography.

Reading the questions helps me a lot in my own work, because it makes me realize how much I live in the past. I'm finishing a novel, *Forbidden Dreams*, in which I have attempted to erase any sense of conventional historical time (and many culturally-specific references) in order to achieve a kind of universal comprehension, independent of language or place, yet retain the sense of hyper-realism.

In my other works, I've found that I have to be very careful to explain even the most innocuous historical references. My children—25, 15 and 12, for example, have no idea what the Karen Silkwood Syndrome is, or Three Mile Island.

I try to write for anyone who has been able to get to, say, the second year of high school. This is a difficult discipline, but I always try to keep in mind the

I looked like the Wolfman on Skid Row.

language of Jesus in Sermon on the Mount, which even in translation 2,000 years later speaks directly to the heart.

By the way, I'd be unworthy of even my small place in the Pynchon industry if I didn't ask whether you ever heard tell of any reaction on his part to "Who [...'the Hell'...— not in title—JS] Is Thomas Pynchon...?

None, as far as I know.

Your title?

Absolutely not. My title was "Do you believe in ESP?" When I got the galleys, all they showed was "Who is Thomas Pynchon" and I corrected the missing question mark. Then the story came out and I was outraged. I called Arthur Kretchmer (*Playboy* Editorial Director) at his home and started *raving.*
  "Will $1,000 make you feel better?" he replied.
  "I feel better already," I answered.
  Worse than the title was the photo of me, which was taken in Mendocino in 1976 after Chrissie and I broke up for good. Pynchon was a big hurdle in our marriage, as she was left very depressed by the experience, but ultimately it was my cheating that caused her to leave me. I was unbelievably blue the day the picture was taken. It was a gray drizzly day and the shot they selected was a little out of focus. I looked like the Wolfman on Skid Row.

This is what you get for vanity.

"Vanity, all is vanity."—Ecclesiastes

From: Jules Siegel <jsiegel@mail.caribe.net.mx>
To: Dkipen@aol.com
Subject: My health

DKIPEN@AOL.COM WROTE: *I'm sorry you haven't been well. Not that hip acting up again, I hope?*

I'm a little slow. "Sitting up and taking a little nourishment," was a joke. Like, still alive here, har–har.

From: Paul Mackin <mackin@allware.com>
Subject: *Re:* Etienne Cherdlu

One can't help wonder if AI researcher Terry Winograd, originator of the famous SHRDLU natural language computer program, was possibly a Pynchon fan.

W's later work (e.g., *Understanding Computers and Cognition,* with Fernando Flores) would lead to a belief that his scope extended far beyond the mathematico-logical paradigm.

From: George Haberberger <ghaberbe@frontiernet.net>
Subject: *Re:* Etienne Cherdlu

Any cryptographer worth his/her salt will tell you that the frequency of letters in the English language is E, then T, then A, then O, …

This is also reflected in the earlier days of moveable type printing, where the E box was the largest.

But then, this doesn't really answer your question, does it?

> *E-mail messages have to translate the myriad character sets in use by the world's languages. Sometimes, they don't get translated very well, as in the example below. This is not a medium for the compulsive copy editor. From here on, I have removed all these artifacts in the interests of readability.*

From: Arne =?unknown-8bit?q?Herl=F8v?= Petersen
         <herlahp@inet.uni-c.dk>
Subject: banana bufotenine

Banana peels contain the alkaloid bufotenine, which can also be found in green peppers. It exists naturally in the human body and in greater amounts in the skin of the common toad (*Bufo bufo bufo*), as well as in certain mushrooms like *Amanita citrina* and *Amanita porphyrea*. It is unlikely that the small amounts of bufotenine in banana peels can create hallucinations. The Danish standard work on hallucinogens by Sten Larris says that no known examples of banana-induced hallucinations are known, although lots of people have tried it and some persons mention great laughing sessions, like those some people experience after smoking pot.

From: David Nevin Friedman <namdeirf@gwis2.circ.gwu.edu>
Subject: *Re:* Banana peels

Speaking of bananas and the East Village, has anyone seen the new Velvet Underground Boxed Set? There is a removable vinyl banana on the cover of the box. Aside from the phallic connotations of a banana (thanks yet again, Freud) does anyone know if the Velvet intended there to be any narcotic effect from bananas?

Subject: *Re:* Etienne Cherdlu
From: David Caesuras <casseres@apple.com>

PAUL MACKIN <MACKIN@ALLWARE.COM> WRITES: *One can't help wonder if AI researcher Terry Winograd, originator of the famous* SHRDLU *natural language computer program, was possibly a Pynchon fan.*

No no. Only a few years ago (well maybe 20), there was nothing unusual about knowing the string ETAOIN SHRDLU. Honest. Not everyone knew it was the top row on a Linotype keyboard but everyone who was literate had seen it many times.

---

tejas@infi.net wrote:

It often showed up in Walt Kelly's "Pogo" comic strip…
                    —Ted Samsel
                    "Took all the money I had in the bank,
                    Bought a rebuilt carburetor, put the rest in the
                    tank." USED CARLOTTA. 1995

An e-mail discussion list is managed by the list's OWNER, *often the person who originated the list. Some lists are* MODERATED—*the owner or his or her representative reviews every message posted to the list and bounces anything that is too long, far off-topic, abusive or otherwise inappropriate. Pynchon-L is an unmoderated list, but its co-owner, Murthy Yenamandra, whom we meet for the first time in the following message, is an active participant. When the discussion gets out of hand, he might step in with a few calming words or a clarification. Andrew Dinn, who administers the Pynchon-L Archive, is also very active on the list, but tends to get a bit more involved in the controversies than Murthy.*

From: Murthy Yenamandra <yenamand@cs.umn.edu>
Subject: *Re:* Banana peels
To: jsiegel@pdc.caribe.net.mx (Jules Siegel)

Hi,

Just wanted to enquire off-list whether you are *the* Jules Siegel of the *Playboy* article fame. If so, thanks for contributing to the few bits of Pynchon biography! In any case, welcome to the list.

> —Murthy pynchon-l co-admin
> Murthy Yenamandra, Dept of CompSci,
> U of Minnesota.
> "Always there's that space between what you feel
> and what you do, and in that gap all human
> sadness lies."   —*Blue Dog*

Lists vary in size and activity, but one statistic is constant, less than 10 per cent of the subscribers contribute regularly. Most subscribers are lurkers, in list-talk. That is, they lurk silently, observing but not contributing. Some lists, such as Mary Anne Mohanraj's Erotica@Cyberia.Com, which is devoted to the art and science of writing literary erotica, discourage lurking and insist that subscribers contribute regularly. I subscribed to Erotica@Cyberia.Com for a while and that was how I found Dale L. Larson. The textual analysis on the list was perhaps even more dense than Pynchon-L@Waste.Org, the literary discussions distinctly more serious. There was a lot less flaming and argument in general and the people were much nicer to each other. The stories, though! I learned so much about knots and gags and whips that I could have hired myself out as an interrogator in some place such as Iraq.

Part 2: A Lurker No More

Richard Romeo <rr.tfcny@mail.fdncenter.org> wrote:

Having met Mr. Pynchon, do you feel that has had any effect in any way on your reading of his work?

JULES REPLIES: This is going to be a rather long reply, because in order to answer your question accurately I have to talk about myself more than about Tom and I also have to present some background on the power politics of linguistic style. Since Arne Herløv Petersen asked me privately for some biographical information, this may not be a complete waste of the group's interest.

If I hadn't known him, I might never have read *V.* I was into W. Somerset Maugham, John O'Hara and John LeCarré, among other novelists. I never liked Faulkner, but read him as a duty. I thought Hemingway was a pompous jerk, but I was enchanted by *Raintree County* by Ross Lockridge, Jr. (a very under-appreciated and complex masterpiece) and *Moby Dick*, so it's not just clarity of style that I go for. My Soho friends used to jeer when I tried to explain to them how great Norman Rockwell was. Robert Grossmann once said very fondly, "Jules, you have a touching nostalgia for reality." All art is abstract art, however. Rockwell is no more realistic than Rauschenberg. He is just more accessible.

I realize that I am condemning myself here to being dismissed as bourgeois and trivial. This may be true, but I see linguistic (and visual) style in terms of power politics. English spelling has never been regularized the way most other modern languages have because it is a tool of class warfare. If you don't learn how to spell English by age 12 or so, you never will, just the way you will never be able to speak a foreign language without an accent if you learn after puberty. I believe that Spanish, Italian and French spelling were regularized under Napoleon in order ease the path to mass literacy.

As with everything British, our deliberately eccentric spelling system is used by the ruling class to maintain the upper hand. Among them:

[1] If you spell impeccably and are not a member of the ruling class, you are a grind.

[2] If you are a member of the lower classes and you can't spell, you deserve to be poor because you were born stupid.

[3] If you are an upper class snot and you can't spell, it's a reflection of your status—you don't have to spell when you are born so well; your servants do it for you.

As you may know, there are two competing systems of English grammar, prescriptive and descriptive. Prescriptive grammar is usually based on the rules of Latin and Greek, which are declined languages—that is, words are inflected to indicate their meaning, as in whom, which is a kind of fossil. Descriptive grammar is based on English as it is used. Modern English is not a declined language but a syntactic language. The position of the word in the sentence tells you what it means. You often cannot understand the word unless you understand the sentence, the paragraph and even the whole work. I am being quite simplistic here, and I will welcome correction by any linguists reading this, but I think that you will find me accurate in outline.

When I was younger, a very Latinate prescriptive grammar was taught in private schools and descriptive grammar was taught in public schools. When I attended Cornell, we were given a freshman English grammar qualifying exam which I failed miserably because I had never heard any of the terms they used. So prescriptive grammar was a kind of invisible affirmative action program for the well-born. I never forgot that bitter lesson, nor did I ever have the luxury of writing very much merely to please. At first, I wrote mostly at the behest of others to promote their points of view. I worked simultaneously in the Nixon and JFK campaigns in 1960. Even as a free-lance writer, I wrote to inform, sometimes to convince.

Writing was almost always an instrument of economic power for me, whether my own or someone else's. I had to struggle very hard to maintain my own sense of self. When I realized that people were reading what I wrote and it was affecting their lives, I tried to be faithful to the truth and to the interests of the class into which I was born. That made me a very difficult writer to deal with. It also made me essentially incapable of truly appreciating the merely decorative in writing. I was irrevocably scarred by the facts of life in our time. I had to take larger and larger doses of amphetamine in order to mediate these contradictions. During the 1970s, I began to give up writing and turned to visual art, writing out books in my own handwriting for the sheer pleasure of the action of writing. Eventually, I gave up defining myself as a writer and turned to graphic design as a profession. Here I am only interested in the decorative and the trivial and I have no pretensions at all and I am much happier for it.

I don't know whether Tom studied prescriptive or descriptive grammar. I do know that despite his family's middle-class economic situation, he had ruling class prejudices and a ruling class higher education which were reflected in his style of writing. He is a decorative writer, as befits his status. His writing is an expression of his sexuality, like the male bird's brilliant plumage. My writing has always been utilitarian, as befits my status as a low-born prole. It is the nest, rather than the song. He once wrote me: "I am a spider, spinning my web out of my own substance. You are a bumblebee, going from flower to flower gathering pollen and nectar." I took this as an insult, but it was a very great compliment.

Summing up: Had I not known him, I would probably have dismissed his work as obscure and essentially useless. I wasn't interested in solving lengthy literary crossword puzzles (although I once astounded a group of students in the Hunter College cafeteria by completing *The New York Times* crossword puzzle in ink). I read his work not because I found it fascinating, but because he was my friend. When he stopped being my friend, I stopped reading his work.

Did you and Pynchon particularly discuss politics during your time together and if so, would you say you were both in agreement on most issues?

We discussed them by mail. I was and am a classic Jewish liberal Democrat and I thought the country was opening up. He was much more astute about this and assured me that it was merely a temporary trend and that it was really closing down.

Also, do you have any idea why he moved to Mexico?

None that I'm willing to put online. He might have liked it because it was so inexpensive here in those days.

> *Chrissie and Robert arrived in Cancun to visit Faera and to vaca-*
> *tion for a couple of weeks. I told them about what I was doing and*
> *proposed that Chrissie answer questions from Pynchon-L. She en-*
> *thusiastically agreed, with the following results. This was also my*
> *first formal announcement that I was indeed "the" Jules Siegel. Now*

Chrissie Jolly, the female point of our ex-triangle

the questions really started flowing in. As it turned out, it was impossible to get all of them answered. As usual, I talked a lot about myself and Chrissie, which some liked and others found egotistical.

From:	Jules Siegel
To:	pynchon-l@waste.org
Re:	Online interview with Chrissie

GREETINGS TEAM PYNCHON!

Yes, I'm the Jules Siegel who wrote the infamous *Playboy* memoir. And, now [… 21-gun salute as jets scream across Cancun crystal skies in—what else?—V-formation …], allow me to present Virginia Christine Wexler, the former Chrissie Jolly, the female point of our ex-triangle. Chrissie is here in Cancun visiting our daughter Faera. She's agreed to try to answer any questions you might have. Try to be brief so that as many members as possible can have a chance.

First question?

Penny Padgett <padgett@intellicorp.com> wrote:

Jules Siegel offers us an opportunity to question one of Pynchon's ex-lovers. I have the uncomfortable feeling I'm being zoomed, here, somehow, but I'll bite. What can you tell me about Pynchon's intense desire for privacy?

JULES: When I published the original *Playboy* piece, someone wrote me a really nasty letter reaming me out for having invaded Tom's privacy. I had to point out that Tom had no problems about invading (indeed, penetrating) my privacy, and then dumping me as a friend. Nor did he consider his caricatures of Chrissie's *persona* invasions of her privacy. Before writing the piece, I informed him by mail that I had the assignment and asked him to speak now or forever hold his peace.

My general impression of Tom is that he's like anyone—he wants his privacy but he also likes publicity. He's certainly gotten himself quite a bit of attention by acting mysterious.

Why don't the two of you share it, either for yourselves or for him?

Chrissie can answer for herself, but I am online here because it's fun and because Andrew Dinn has encouraged me to share my thoughts.

Andrew Dinn speculated on my motives for writing the *Playboy* memoir, "And it looks from the outside as if much of the motive in doing so was anger and resentment because of what happened between him and Chrissie." I think my answer to him is worth repeating here:

The motive was professional. Anger and resentment had nothing to do with it. Sex was quite communal in those days. Do you think he was Chrissie's only fling? I remained friendly with a couple of others, in the full knowledge that they had been fooling around in the bushes. Of course, I got angry. She got angry when I cheated on her. But sex was sex, and friendship was friendship. Whatever happened between the two of them was just something that happened to a lot of friends, especially at that time. Some remained friends. He was incapable of that. He chose to terminate the friendship, not I. Once he was no longer a friend, I had no reason to refrain from converting what I knew about him into a very affectionate and flattering memoir that happened also to bring me the literary attention I needed at the time—which was its only point in the first place.

I personally feel that privacy is an illusion of the ego and a function of industrialism and capitalism. Historically, it's a very late arrival on the human scene, and, I think, often pernicious. If you had to live your life completely transparently, how would you act?

Interesting. I'm interested in your argument that Pynchon makes a big deal about his privacy in order to garner publicity. Publicity may be an agreeable side effect of his efforts to guard his privacy, but I can't believe that it's the only reason he does it.

I'm not saying that. See below.

After all, going to such lengths is a lot of work, no?

Not in terms of the pay-off. See below

In true paranoid style, I fear that your "completely transparent" scenario may arrive sooner rather than later.

Don't be afraid. It already has pretty much for me and it is good for the most part, not bad. Do you want telepathy and oneness with the universe, or do you want a police state? That's really the choice. I, too, hate the thought of my stupid actions of the past being exposed to public ridicule. Every once in a while, I remember another moronic moment that I wish I could just erase. Sometimes I tell them to Anita (my beautiful wife), and she laughs and I feel a rush of self-forgiveness.

J. P. Donleavy once said, "Writing is turning your worst moments into money." I think our job is to create a world in which it is possible for people to enjoy living transparently. We have to eliminate these silly taboos and absurd laws. It's really all about poo-poo and pee-pee and titty—but our need for dignity (and familial and economic competition in what we are taught is a zero-sum universe) lead us into many regrettable and sometimes ugly situations. We need to cultivate bravery and tolerance. If we have an enemy, it is shame itself, the most powerful weapon of control and repression.

I look forward to hearing from Chrissie as well.

> *A gap of a day or so intervened. I took Faera's laptop over to the hotel Chrissie and Robert were staying in and I repeated Penny's questions and the others that had arrived in the interim. Chrissie was in excellent spirits. She likes coming to Cancun to see Faera, as she and Robert live in Houston, where he is Manager of Information Systems for a major oil company. As you get to know Chrissie here, you will understand how it must seem to her in the vast suburbs, no matter how luxurious her life might be. I later edited these questions and answers into the more conversational flow that follows.*

JULES: She's right here with me now. How do you feel about Pynchon's privacy needs, Chrissie?

CHRISSIE: He didn't want people to know that his family was poor and so was he. They were aristocrats in Oyster Bay, but they didn't have any money and I feel that his mother wanted people to think they were rich anyway. In those days—the Fifties—it was important for upper class people to have money as well as being socially upper crust. But now, in the Nineties, everything has changed. Now movie stars are making money and they're not from the upper classes and it's not as important. It's more important to be self-made. And he is. So he's holding on to something for no good reason.

JULES: Well, what about Penny's point about cooperating in maintaining his privacy?

CHRISSIE: The stuff I'm revealing is pretty tame. It's universal. He doesn't realize that the stuff he gets upset about isn't scandalous. It's generic. I don't know any family in that class that doesn't have the same problems. They suffer from reverse discrimination because of their last names. It doesn't help them. It goes against them.

What I was really interested in hearing about is why is Pynchon so hell-bent on staying out of the public eye?

CHRISSIE: Because he doesn't have time to write and concentrate on the public eye at the same time. He writes at night and he's very tired during the day and he's never been very physically strong. His health was always poor when I knew him.

Look at what the press did to the Royal Family. Look how they made their lives a shambles. They completely destroyed their image throughout the world. The press makes money off people. They can sell more copies if they write about him because he's mysterious. He feels they're making money off him as a kind of free lunch. There are so many scam artists in the newspaper racket. The press is very toxic. They make up lies about your private life. He's trying to protect himself from them.

It's a license to steal money, writing those books. He doesn't want anyone interfering, especially the dumb, annoying people that are out there in the world.

JULES: I think he's a fearful person who also has secrets he doesn't want anyone to stumble across. He once said something to me to the effect that paranoids aren't paranoid by nature, but they do things that make them paranoid. I remember him as a good Catholic boy who went to Mass, so maybe all he's talking about are his sins. He had very severe orthodontic problems that undoubtedly inspired his psychodontics satire in *V.* When I knew him his molars were grotesquely malformed and his front teeth were too large for his jaw, giving him a chipmunk face. I think the combination of his Catholic upbringing and his dental problems made him fearful of facing new people.

Creating a Scarlet Pimpernel persona would seem to compensate for the lack of seriousness of the chipmunk effect. We all want dignity. Being mysterious attracts attention in a James Bond sort of way without seeming to grovel for it.

Despite this, I always thought Tom was quite handsome, until he wrote me a letter commenting on his teeth and I began to realize how this all must have felt from the inside out. I've always been reluctant to write about this, because I didn't want to hurt him, but sometimes I think that maybe it might help him, too.

O N HIS FATHER'S SIDE, his heritage is 100% New England, and I think this created other inhibitions about exposure. He doesn't want to be judged or ridiculed, and I have to say I don't blame him. I am quite reluctant to be interviewed except on my own terms and I had good reason to regret the exposure I once eagerly welcomed when I was in the public eye. People are crazy. There's more than one Charles Manson out there. This past thirty years have certainly confirmed Tom's fears. People who smoked grass or took other illegal drugs had a lot to think about, didn't we? There was always the fear of the knock on the door.

I also think that the obsession serves his need for publicity very well. If he's a writer he's got to be in it for the fame as well as the money, right? So he's turned his obsession into a great gimmick. He has added economic value to his persona by making it hard to get. This is very close to what psychoanalysts call the highly compensated neurosis. I'm sure he didn't plan this out. He does know how to make the most of it.

To what extent does this desire of his impinge on his friends? Are they, in effect, sworn to secrecy? ("Those who know don't tell, and those who tell don't know.")

CHRISSIE: If you know someone who has an IQ of a certain level, a word to the wise is sufficient. If you're going to hang out with someone who's really smart, you're going to be smart, too, and you're going to be a quick study. You're going to pick up on the fact that he doesn't want anyone to know anything, period.

JULES: I never knew any of his friends. The secrecy never affected me at all. I wrote about him and his work on a couple of occasions when I felt like it and he never complained.

He cut me off during his scene with Chrissie, not after I wrote the profile.

What, if anything, does it say about his art?

CHRISSIE: He can write about his friends and if no one knows who they are they won't be able to analyze this. It's easier to keep track of your characters if you base them on your friends. It's a convenient way to write. He doesn't want people to know that he's doing this.

JULES: The over-elaboration of detail is often an expression of acute anxiety. One sees this when over-dosing on amphetamine, which creates a similar effect, including the paranoia, I think because it is similar to adrenaline, which produces similar symptoms. The acutely anxious person produces many stress hormones as part of the attempt to mediate the pain by performing miracles. Over-stimulation leads to injudicious actions, too. When you crash, you experience a profound paranoid depression as you review your errors rather than your triumphs. I see this tone of deep regret in much of his work. His story "Low-Lands," is as much about regret and depression as it is about physics. So is *Gravity's Rainbow*, from the little of it I skimmed.

John Mascaro <mascaro@humnet.ucla.edu> wrote:

This interview thing is fascinating, if confusing. I don't quite understand if this is an open conversation or who's exactly talking to whom, but that's never stopped me from blundering in before.

JULES: Maybe it should.

JOHN: I would like to protest that this—drug theory—of P.'s work is preposterously reductive and mechanistic. It completely smears over the individual response to chemical interaction. You seem to tar P w/ that brush in your *Playboy* article too, which I haven't reread in years, so maybe I am misremembering.

JULES: I will appreciate your reading the material carefully before offering hostile opinions off the top of your head.

JOHN: Aren't you (if it is Mr. Siegal I am addressing) the source of that infamous statement about his writing *Gravity's Rainbow* while being totally wasted?

JULES: You are speaking directly with Jules Siegel, the author of the infamous *Playboy* memoir about Thomas Pynchon. My ex-wife, Chrissie Wexler, is visiting us in Cancun and she agreed to be interviewed online.

JOHN: I don't think I have ever read P. himself attest to this anywhere. Actually, in case I am wrong about the source, does anybody know the source of that assertion?

JULES: He told me so directly himself. We usually smoked grass together when I visited California.

JOHN: But the idea that Dangerous Drugs actually—wrote—Thomas Pynchon, well, it's downright Rushdian.

JULES: I didn't say that drugs wrote Thomas Pynchon. I said that he himself commented directly to me that he had to re-write quite a bit of *Gravity's Rainbow* because he was so wasted when he wrote the draft that he couldn't understand what he might have meant.

I am not speaking directly of drug use here, as obvious from the text, but about the similarities among natural states of acute anxiety and the various effects of drugs such as amphetamine. I am doing this not to tar Tom with any brush but to communicate the state of mind I feel he (we all) often experience, whether writing or not. I don't know if he used amphetamines. I do know that almost all writers of our generation frequently used large quantities of it and I would be surprised to find out that he didn't.

Are you with the DEA? Do you have some kind of prejudice against drugs? If you want to understand the past thirty years, I suggest you put aside your moralistic tone and try to empathize with what we saw, rather than lecturing us about its social connotations.

JOHN: No, I am not with the DEA. Are you? No, I am not moralistically criticizing drugs. I thought the moralism was coming from you, but you deny implying or asserting in your post that you see P.'s creativity as a—symptom—of his drug use. I say you—are—making the implication, and that in fact it IS a moralistic one, on your part.

I also wonder how you can chide me to read—your—posts carefully while admitting to having only skimmed parts of *Gravity's Rainbow*. Pretty silly of you, isn't it? I also think you ought to read your own posts carefully, because it looks like you contradict yourself twice; once when you write a paragraph about drug reactions and say it's not about drug reactions, and again when you say you are not the source of the Infamous Drug Confession, because P. told you himself (did I read that right? is this what you are saying?)

But of course you are the source of the Infamous Drug Confession, since I never read P. himself ever say he told you anything. But, please, I am not being hostile, though I think there is hostility in what you write, especially about P. (and I always wonder—why?), I was just welcoming you to the list in the spirit of true drug-addled anarchic flame-throwing fun. Maybe you'll stick around long enough to decide it's time to actually read him.

P.S. If I told you how many times I have watched my dead grandmother crawl up my leg with a knife between her teeth, would you believe I have nothing against a little drug use?

—jm

JULES: [1] I didn't deny being the source of the dope quote. I affirmed it. It's in the article.

[2] Please be specific about my "hostility."

[3] I'm not analyzing *Gravity's Rainbow*. I'm offering opinions about the psychological sources of Tom's writing style and personal style and I am very careful to point out the gaps in my knowledge.

[4] Comparing stress hormones to drugs is not saying they are the same thing. Please read this over again and try to understand what I am saying. I am not moralizing about drug use nor am I saying that his style is a symptom of drug use. I defy anyone to accurately identify drug-induced writing. A writer friend, Craig Vetter, once complained that he didn't like what I wrote on amphetamine. I asked him what piece he liked least. "Alpha machines in *Penthouse*," he replied. Written on a cup of coffee. Most? "Family Secrets." *New American Review #10*. The result of the single largest dose of amphetamine I took in my entire life. At the same time, I think it very fair and useful to discuss modern culture in terms of drug use, for better or worse.

[5] My name is spelled Siegel.

[6] I am not sure what your statement about your grandmother means. Did this really happen? Are you talking about drug-induced hallucinations? If you are, I think that it would be useful for you to examine the source of the pain it expresses with someone you trust deeply.

[7] I read all his short stories. I read *V.* carefully more than once and I summarized it for North American Newspaper Alliance in 1963. *The Crying of Lot 49* left me cold, but I did read it. From what I see here, many of the people

on the list have not been able to get through *Gravity's Rainbow* and, in fact, are here in order to understand it better.

I'm sure you're sincere in your views, but it would be helpful if you would slow down a little and organize your thoughts more carefully, as they are difficult for me to answer in their present form. Everything that I write here is carefully considered and edited before I send it out. I enjoy this, but it's quite a bit of work and I think it merits your respect.

---

tstanton@nationalgeographic.com wrote:

I have always chuckled at what sounds like indignation over the fact TRP might have smoked a little pot to fuel the writing process, and the gullibility of anyone who believed the brag "I was so fucked up I dunno what I was doing, but it was brilliant when I did it…"

Let's get real folks. Writers, poets, painters, *et. al.* have abused "substances" & created great work, whether on the substance or as an after effect. People who make their living critiquing these works don't usually want to brag to their peers that the subject of their thesis or book is a confirmed pot head (although I find the insider drug jokes funny & one of GR's more endearing qualities). Conversely, anyone who has done more than "skimmed" *Gravity's Rainbow* cannot dismiss it as the ravings of a paranoid pot head, except from pure meanness.

Gravity's Rainbow is a heavily crafted work of art that you may like or dismiss on its own merits. The art world is full of alcoholics, addicts, wife beaters, and other abusers, but the one quality they possessed was the ability to create great work in spite of (or as a consequence of) their respective afflictions. If TRP's only crime was rollin' up a splif to loosen up his Puritanical upbringing, he would be no worse than millions of us who did precisely the same thing during the Seventies & beyond.

JULES: Hear! Hear!

MantaRay@aol.com writes:

Hey, I read the entire thing stoned, why shouldn't TPynchon get to write it all that way? No wonder it made total sense!!

Andrew Dinn <andrew@cee.hw.ac.uk> wrote:

That's no joke. One of my major motives for conducting the GRGR at such a slow pace was a stoned read of *Gravity's Rainbow*. Instead of rushing through the book at my usual frantic pace I was slowed down enough that I began to see the beauty of the language, the craft in the construction and the many levels of interconnectedness— words, ideas, themes, events etc. Doubtless one can arrive at such by other means but I think I'll take the high road....

JULES: Heartily agree here. I remember the first time I heard Bob Dylan while stoned in 1964. Everything became clarified. We are all mostly in highly accelerated states of consciousness because of the forced-march pace of our survival struggle. The artist creates his world one stroke at a time. I thought Chrissie's comments about Tom's frame by frame technique important. He's like Spenser, very mediaeval in his approach—panel after panel of illuminated tableaux. We don't know how *The Faerie Queen* read to contemporaries in its time. Could be lots of finger-poppin' there that we can't appreciate. Same with Tom.

JOHN: O.K., Mr. Siegal (sorry about the misspelling). You read your things, I'll read mine. I won't engage in a point by point commentary on your point-by-point commentary because that will get us nowhere. I will also continue to post without carefully revising and editing because that's what I think this list is for, though I admit it gets me in trouble sometimes.

I really do think that you sometimes go way too far in presuming knowledge of P. and his work, and I will say forthrightly that I feel a hostility from you towards him that further complicates your motives in acting as this odd sort of midwife or go between, this Gatekeeper of Authenticity. But my brothers and sisters of the list seem to dig what you are doing, with some reservations, so that's cool.

P.S. The revelation about my grandmom should have been self-evident, though I guess your need to psychoanalyze just got in the way again. And it just occurs to me that maybe that's what bugs me about your enterprise: it reduces to a kind of psychoanalytic criticism, and that's just never been my cup of meat. It has always been a school of criticism noted for hostility towards its subjects, btw.

Part 3:
A Midnight Visit
with the Werewolf

From: Jules Siegel <jsiegel@mail.caribe.net.mx>
To: pynchon-l@waste.org
Subject: A Midnight Visit with the Werewolf

[Screen fills with garbage characters morphing into a web browser down-loading mail, an innocent lad's face lighted only by the eerie CRT glow, his eyes fixed on the scrolling lines as if seeking relief from the flickering image of Grandma standing in the shadows, a hint of something shiny and sharp in her hand.]

mascaro@humnet.ucla.edu wrote:

O.K., Mr. Siegal (sorry about the misspelling).

JULES: Don't be sorry, son. Be correct. You got it wrong again. And call me Jules. I'm not your high school English teacher. I'm a gnarly old literary werewolf with fangs and claws. The moon is full tonight and grandma is your baby-sitter. "Oh, hi, Mr. Werewolf." Sounds silly. So does Jules, but Yehudah is worse. That's my real name. Yehudah ben Eli Sagon Halevi. Most Jews of my generation had Hebrew names but were given American names on their birth certificates. My birth certificate reads "Baby Siegel" because my mother and father couldn't agree on a name. My mother wanted Julian. My father insisted on Julius. Everyone called me Julie or Yüdel. I didn't know my name was Jules until I went to pre-school. I insisted my name was Julius and they had to call my mother on the phone to get me to shut up about it. You talk about argumentative people! No wonder I love the Internet. One big raving argument. Home at last, Lord, I am home at last!

You read your things, I'll read mine.

Afraid to open your eyes, puppy? Maybe you better close the blinds and pull the covers over your head, too. The werewolf is howling for blood tonight. You think Grandma's bad? Wait until you see my shadow on your bedroom wall. Yowwwwwww! Lon Chaney was an actor. I am a fugitive from the brain gang, all teeth and no mind.

[**Blood-chilling laughter, followed by loud snorting and panting as if sniffing the air to locate victim, then steely claws scratching at the window with a squeal worse than galvanized 10-penny nails on a polished marble crypt.**]

I won't engage in a point by point commentary on your point-by-point commentary because that will get us nowhere.

It will get us somewhere if you try to be serious and make an effort to understand what I'm saying rather than reacting from your own off-the-wall perceptions. Here's a challenge: I say you won't do it because you can't. You know that the things you say are often just things that you say. When you run into a rusty chain saw like me, you fold your arms and look at the ceiling and retreat into haughty boredom. If I'm wrong about this, prove it by responding with stuff that merits our consideration. You never know, we might learn something. I'm more than open to correction where I'm wrong. Are you?

I will also continue to post without carefully revising and editing because that's what I think this list is for, though I admit it gets me in trouble sometimes.

Very mature. I admire your creative command of the anal aggressive character. Obstinate and messy, rather than obstinate and neat, as in the anal retentive. The list is for discussing Tom's work and anything else that the members feel pertinent. Your style of doing so is your own choice. In the present instance, it enables you to make antagonistic and unfair statements (which, frankly, make me feel bad when I read them) and then to back off by acting gooney when I try reasonable interpretations. This isn't being cute. It's slovenly. It wastes people's time. It creates confusion. Please try to remember to use your Pampers next time you have to go out in public.

I really do think that you sometimes go way too far in presuming knowledge of P. and his work

I don't presume anything. I write from direct knowledge. My opinions are clearly labeled as opinion, my inferences as inference, and the gaps in my direct knowledge are clearly indicated as well.

I will say forthrightly that I feel a hostility from you towards him…

You can forthrightly tell us where you see *any* hostility in my comments about Tom. Put up or shut up. If you're wrong, you can be civilized and apologize. Just because you're online doesn't mean that you have the unrestricted right to kick others around with unsupported attacks like this. If you perceive hostility in this reply, you've finally got something right. It is directed at you, because of the unfairness of your accusations and your generally unreasonable tone. I'm sure that you get off on reactions like this. Since I'm really a nice werewolf, I'm giving you what you want rather than ignoring you. Makes me sad to see a fellow work so hard at being annoying and not get the full benefit of his investment.

…that further complicates your motives…

My motives are quite clear: I am enjoying the interaction with the list and I welcome the public attention after so many years of isolation here in Cancun, a resort built and operated for human robots by human robots. We did have a Comedy Club here, but it went out of business before the authorities could shut it down. We do a big business with humor impaired groups. Probably the only resort in the world that is fully fitted out for this segment of the handicapped. Could be a big market for humor implants, too. Had your humor implant yet, boy?

…in acting as this odd sort of midwife or go between, this Gatekeeper of Authenticity…

This is arrant name-calling. No cross-dressing allowed here either. I am a guy. Don't make me have to remind you again. Midwife is a sexist term. See alt.lib.male. I like the Gatekeeper of Authenticity, though. What does the uniform look like? Lots of blue serge and brass buttons, I hope. And a portable CB. Got to have a CB to summon the Reality Squad when distortionists get nasty.

p.s. the revelation about my grandmom should have been self-evident

It wasn't. Please explain what you meant. Did your grandmom attack you with an ax? You should have reported her to the authorities. I think this would definitely be considered child abuse in most jurisdictions. Or is this something you hallucinate when engaging in substance abuse and you were trying express solidarity with other casualties of the Psychedelic Revolution by telling me this?

I guess your need to psychoanalyze just got in the way again.

I don't have a need to psychoanalyze. It's just one of the techniques I use to explain feelings and their sources. I didn't psychoanalyze your statement. I reacted compassionately to what I perceived to be the pain expressed in it by suggesting that you examine the source. Darn, I'm naive. You were just funning, weren't you?

And it just occurs to me that maybe that's what bugs me about your enterprise: it reduces to a kind of psychoanalytic criticism

It doesn't reduce to anything like that at all. What bugs you is my magisterial tone and my disrespectful manner of talking about your hero as if he were merely another guy, a great artist, but just another guy. This goes for some others, too. When I told Anita about the guilt trippers, she said, "They're afraid Pynchon might be reading all this and they don't want to get in trouble."

Tom—are you there, Tom? Did you get the names of the traitors who admitted to enjoying all this? Hah-hah! Another great sting operation. Any of you guys read about the fake re-mail services run by the intelligence agencies? This is the absolute truth and may God strike me dead with a thunderbolt if I lie. Government intelligence agents set up re-mail services in order to spy on the people using them. We're watching you, Pynchon fans. Tom knows who you are. He's studying you for his next book.

It has always been a school of criticism noted for hostility towards its subjects, BTW.

BTW? Bacon and tomato on white toast? I'll have one, too, real crispy on the bacon please and lots of mayonnaise. I assume you're talking about literary psychoanalysis. I haven't read any of it, so I have to plead ignorance here. Be good to hear you plead a little ignorance, too.

Anyone agree? Or am I being too rough on the lad? Imagine that. Me, a mere newcomer to this list, talking back harshly to a young old hand. Deserve whatever I get, right? Excuse me, it's getting late and I have to go make sure the firewall is shut down tight. Never know when some nutball is going to take umbrage. Took a lot of umbrage myself back when. Looked like yellow pumpkin seeds, didn't it?

[Exit Werewolf, talking to himself and waving his arms, followed by the sound of the firewall slamming shut with a loud thunk like a ship's hatch.]

> *For the non-Internet-literate: a firewall is a computer networking setup designed to keep intruders, such as hackers, out of the corporate system. "BTW" means "By the way." As you can see, I wasn't very experienced with this terminology myself when this began, although I did know what BTW meant. I was just having a little fun here.*

---

ghaberbe@frontiernet.net wrote:

JULES WROTE: *"[6] I am not sure what your statement about your grandmother means. Did this really happen? Are you talking about drug-induced hallucinations? If you are, I think that it would be useful for you to examine the source of the pain it expresses with someone you trust deeply."*

This is an allusion to Hunter S. Thompson's *Fear and Loathing in Las Vegas.*
—George Haberberger

JULES REPLIES: Thanks, George. Never been much of a Hunter S. Thomspon fan, as I always felt he gave drugs a bad name, as well as encouraging by example stupid overdosing, mixing the wrong things, and generally abusing substances that are really antidotes to the general horror of our time. He wasn't a psychedelic prophet, he was a tawdry glutton.

As they say in Mexican alcohol announcements, *"Todo en medida; nada en exceso."*—Everything in measure, nothing in excess. I don't think that applies to art, necessarily, or love, or sensuality, but it sure applies to these potentially very toxic potions we use to survive the disgusting insults we are subjected to every day: smog, crowding, hate, noise...*ad infinitum*. Very little of that here; consequently very little drug abuse—although kids will be kids.

I feel it's very important to post this message. When I describe our drug use in the Sixties and Seventies, I am not recommending it, neither directly nor by inference. I myself fell into problems with alcohol when I was at Cornell because I thought that's what college and writing was all about, thanks to F. Scott Fitzgerald and others. My anecdotes are there to amuse and instruct, not to glorify.

Henry M <gravity@dcez.nicom.com> wrote:

Jules—I gotta admit, I had my doubts. Not having read any of your writing other than on the list, I really wasn't all that impressed (I believe that you, as most writers, aren't "above" desiring to impress people.) until the werewolf showed his teeth.

Good'ne. I say it's a keeper.

Joe Varo <vjvaro@erie.net> wrote:

I don't know how long you've been a part of the "online" world, Mr. Siegel, but you've pretty much picked up on a major aspect of the 'net, i.e. it's "one big raving argument." Though usually we don't have any major attempts at character assassination here on Pynchon-L and things tend to stay pretty much civil, though often heated.

Again, this is characteristic with this new form of communication. With the anonymous veneer of electrons and ascii, foax are more prone to be far more brazen, disrespectful and flame-happy than in other forms of communication.

Apparently, (and unfortunately) many people *do* believe that being online gives them just this right.

Arne Herløv Petersen <herlahp@inet.uni-c.dk> wrote:

I would like to ask Chrissie about how they met.

CHRISSIE: I was living with Jules in Laurel Canyon in 1966 and we went to visit Tom where he lived in Manhattan Beach and we had a good time sitting around smoking some really strong grass that Jules and I scored at a be-in. We thought the be-in was very odd. It was just a hundred or so people sitting around on the grass in Griffith Park asking themselves why they were there. Next scene.

What happened?

Then in 1968, Jules was in the hospital and Tom was dating my best friend, Susan Gordon of San Marino, and he came over to visit me as a friend and we talked about having an affair, and then about two years later, I was in Los Angeles and Jules was in New York interviewing Herman Kahn, and Tom and I got together in Manhattan Beach. I returned to New York and planned to leave Jules and go back to California with Tom. But the next time I saw him I was three months pregnant and we went to a coffee shop on Sunset Strip and all we talked about was his professional plans for the future.

Why did you break up?

One of the issues between Jules and me was that I wanted a baby right away and Jules didn't. Tom seemed too kooky to have a baby with. Jules came around to my point of view about the baby and I dropped Tom to have the baby with Jules. Look what I got. Look at Faera. Look how special she is. It was a good combination. Tom matured very late. He wasn't as mature as Jules. It was a good time to have a baby. The country was still coming out of that affluent period. People didn't have that feeling of being squeezed for every penny the way they do now. It was still O.K. to be a hippie then. It wasn't as materialistic. As the country got poorer, the people got more uptight. Then the Reagan thing—what a terrible period. It was a lot more laid-back then. It was more like Polynesia. Now it's like Germany.

The hippies tried to steer it in the right direction but they were too irresponsible and they tried to change the institutions too fast for the middle and lower classes. There was a big backlash. They were frightened and jealous. That's what Thomas Pynchon's books are about—the backlash and the resentment about food stamps on both sides; food stamps put labels on people, they were shame-based—and the loss of sentimentality among families and lovers. It's as if the culture had a surgeon come in and cut out the part of the heart that was the source of feelings of sentimentality. People had to give up cherishing each other in order to protect themselves against a new virulent strain of killer bee humans, the young barbarians, the preppies, the white male preppies on Wall Street and their merger and acquisition jobs. They gave up poetry too along the way. Poets are an endangered species. That's what Tom wanted to be, a poet.

I stayed with Jules because he was the poet and the hippie. We actually lived in a commune. We weren't pretending. We were the real thing. Tom didn't stick his neck out and live the way he wrote. He was a classic master artist who stayed home with his four hundred coffee cans and wrote. He was Thrifty MacPynchon. He used to have peanut butter and jelly in his refrigerator so he could save money on food. He didn't like it that I went to the fancy butcher, because it was more expensive than the supermarket.

Do you still see him?

No. I talk to him from time to time on the phone. It averages out about once every three years at Christmas.

Where he is living?

I believe in downtown New York, Soho, in a loft.

How he is as a person?

He's happy now. He's a doting father and he says his wife is "on the sunny side of forty."

I have heard a number of stories telling either that he is completely spaced out, that he always carries his toy animals.

He doesn't carry toy animals around. He has a large collection of statues of pigs and piggy banks. He collects porcelain and clay pigs. People give them to him. He likes the animal. He thinks it's a nice animal. He likes *Charlotte's Web.* He gave me a copy of it and autographed it. He identifies with the pig in *Charlotte's Web.* He doesn't believe in eating pigs either. He thinks pork tastes like human flesh and it would be cannibalism to eat pork. He thinks humans are a lot like pigs.

Does he have a lot of strange quirks?

He's very conventional and old-fashioned and has the values of his generation of the Fifties from upper class Oyster Bay. He never met a person who said

'He's writing cartoons instead of drawing them. They're not two-dimensional, but holograms. They're real people who go in and out of being cartoons.'

"dig" or "man" or "it's not my bag." It's only in his imagination. He'd like to be one of his characters and wear a black leather jacket and stand on the corner and spit. Or he'd like to be one of those surfers that he studied like a sociologist in Manhattan Beach.

He's really a professional sociologist, studying people.

He identifies with the stuttering pig in Looney Tunes—"Th..th..thhatt's all folks!"—because he has a severe stutter when he tries to speak in public. He's trying to do in his books what Warren Beatty did in the film "Dick Tracy." The characters in his books are all cartoon characters. He writes in frames just like a comic strip. He's writing cartoons instead of drawing them. They're not two dimensional but holograms. They're real people who go in and out of being cartoons. They go back and forth between the real world and the cartoon world.

He is a Yankee, a New Englander—wear it out, make it do, or do without.

He needs to follow the Calvinist work ethic in order not to feel guilt about his life. He has to measure up to the Yankee ideal. It's all Newport, Rhode Island stuff, the old WASP combined with the inward-looking Irish Catholic. He's a conservative old-fashioned workaholic with good values, strict Anglo-Christian values. He just happens to be a conservative artist instead of a conservative investment banker.

---

tstanton@nationalgeographic.com wrote:

After reading several of Chrissie's responses I have to say I feel slightly ashamed to have broached TRP's privacy, no matter how "tame" the topics may appear. Yet in the same moment I'm fascinated and not at all surprised to find he's not too far off from what I imagined. You don't get to that level by living—Joyce's family suffered,

Faulkner, etc., the list is endless—but by dedicating yourself to the work. It paid off in the end. TRP has raised the family name back to its aristocratic greatness, has avoided the pitfalls of publicity that drain our artists (involuntarily or in the worst of Warholishness), and managed in the process to significantly change people (just look at this list, and remember we're the vocal ones!). I'm happy he's a doting father (being one myself I can attest it changes you) and I hope *Mason & Dixon* is a crowning achievement for him and his readers. The rest is just a footnote, but I admit to reading every one of them.

—Tom Stanton
Guilty in DC

JULES: As Melvin B. Shestack once said, "This is like feeling guilty about thinking about jerking off." Our material is thirty years old, for the most part. I think Tom would have a lot more fun if he came down off his pedestal and mixed in with the folks, but that's not his idea of fun. Meanwhile, his privacy really does remain intact here so far. This is hardly *People* Magazine. I heard he's relaxed a bit on the privacy obsession. I wouldn't be surprised to see some highly-laundered personal editorial coverage in connection with his new book.

MantaRay@aol.com wrote:

I would just like to say thanks to Chrissie for the info. I had a heart attack laughing at your posting. Especially, the pigs. If I have my cousin dress up as a huge pig in Halloween in Soho, will TRP be magnetically drawn towards him?

I don't mean this to be rude, but when I saw Crumb, his physicality reminded me of what I thought Pynchon might be like (If anyone thinks that's a slam, I personally thought Crumb was cool, so eat it). But now the mention of the pig fetish totally recalls Crumb's leg fetish.

Thanks again for the insights.

—Scott
Berkeley, CA

JULES: Crumb and Pynchon are very close matches physically. They probably come from similar genetic stock.

Pynchon doesn't have a pig fetish (a negatively-charged psychoanalytic term), though. He just collects pigs. I think his opinions about them (which date

It's not easy being an idiot savant, heavy on the idiot.

back to the late Sixties) are a take on the use of the word to mean police. He was defending the kindly, decent pig, see?

Crumb does have a leg fetish—specifically for heavy, muscular female legs. He wrote to me about it once at length in his own handwriting.

I have been a Crumb fanatic since 1967, when I bought his tabloid *Yarrowstalks* in the East Village. No one documented our time with his fidelity to physical detail and psychic environment. Unbelievably great artist, technically, and a humorist who will rank someday with Mark Twain, I think, although the very concreteness of his work may cause him to become too obscure with the passage of time.

He visited us in 1971 when we were living in the commune. *Playboy* had decided to do an Annie Fanny on communes, so Harvey Kurzman showed up with Crumb and Gilbert Spain to do research. They all drew in my first calligraphic journal, *Record*.

Crumb did a spectacular drawing of Chrissie on a separate sheet, which I submitted to *Rolling Stone* as part of a major piece on dope-dealing I was working on for them. Wenner rejected the story (having just begun his full sell-out trajectory, he wanted a hard-hitting expose of nasty gun-toting longhairs—hardly what he got) but kept the drawing. Chrissie is still righteously annoyed that I ever sent him the original in the first place. I have always been the dumb one. As long as I followed her advice about my career I prospered mightily. When I failed to consult her, my native ineptness took over. Anita—classic MYOB WASP—prudently tries to stay out of my professional decisions, but fortunately I have my children to guide me.

It's not easy being an idiot savant, heavy on the idiot.

Ted Samsel <tejas@infi.net> wrote:

Gilbert Spain? Or do you mean Gilbert Shelton or Spain Rodriguez?

JULES: Oops. Both. I think they might have both been there, but I'll have to consult the journal in question.

ckaratnytsky@nypl.org wrote:

Dear Guilty in DC,

Just wanted to let you know that I was glad to read your recent comments re the online interview with Chrissie. I share your feelings. I have been concerned that I have been giving in to my baser instincts by reading the interview—and I disagree, btw, with Jules that this is like feeling guilty about jerking off.

  For me, it's a matter of not liking the fact that I've done something that I know is unkind or unpleasant or distasteful to someone who has made their feelings/wishes about it clear.

  Not feelin' holier than thou here, just a bit regretful...
                          —Guilty in NY, Chris

tstanton@nationalgeographic.com wrote:

CKARATNYTSKY WROTE: *I disagree, btw, with Jules that this is like feeling guilty about jerking off....*

Well, that was a *funny line* so I gotta give it to Jules & Chrissie. One love. Still feels funny, but then so can jerkin' off...

Not feelin' holier than thou here, just a bit regretful...

Agreed, but we'll get over it...

                          —Tom Stanton

Greg Montalbano <opsgmm@uccvma.ucop.edu> wrote:

Perhaps the more sensitive of us would feel better about all of this if we kept the questions on the level of the literary & the scholarly—other authors he may have read/ liked, influences, opinions on, etc.—and left the People Magazine *material alone.*

JULES: I think people should ask the questions they feel like asking. I also very firmly believe that any feelings of guilt or embarrassment are absolutely silly.

Perhaps when we get Chrissie back here and she answers the questions about the models for his characters, she can comment about how she feels about having been repeatedly caricatured. How about me? I haven't looked myself up in his work, but the fact that he might have changed my name and mixed in some other parts of other people doesn't change the facts. He used us. He didn't ask our permission. We didn't get all huffy about it. It was no big deal.

Let me assure you that I am just as concerned about my privacy as Tom is. From time to time, I would have a remission from the obsession and cooperate fully in publicizing some book or *Playboy* article, principally by doing phone-in interviews, but I have never allowed myself to be photographed by any but a *Playboy* photographer, among other restrictions.

At the same time, I do like seeing my name in print and I do welcome the commercial effect this has. The world is dangerous. I have three children. My life has been threatened more than once because of what I've written. I once had to live with an armed guard patrolling outside my window because someone with a gun came out looking to kill me because he didn't like something I wrote about James Taylor.

I'm sure that Tom, who is much more self-protective than even I, would not be at all offended by our analysis. Although we never talked about it, I feel confident that he was concerned about being ridiculed, not appreciated, as we are doing here. His personal security is in no way being compromised.

Henry M <gravity@dcez.nicom.com>

Tom—

If I may call you Tom. If you are lurking or using a cybername. I didn't ask any questions. I didn't ask what was so attractive about you that a woman would cuckold her husband. I didn't ask if you were an attentive lover. I didn't ask…

Bilge Ebiri <Ebiri1@aol.com> wrote:

Hey,

First off, lemme say that I don't have any qualms about finding all this stuff about TRP. I think it seems that the majority of those on this list are fairly responsible readers, academics, students, and generally people who ought to

JUST A LITTLE NOTE FROM THE FOLKS
By R. Crumb

Original ink drawing 16 cm. by 14 cm. in Jules Siegel's *Record* ledger
June 6, 1970, The Chinese House, Lagunitas, Calif.

Record was my first ledger, purchased in Goldsmith's Stationers in Brooklyn Heights on February 13, 1970 to make notes for a novel that had been commissioned by New American Library. Now called *Forbidden Dreams, Fragments of a Novel in Progress*, it is about half finished. Soon after I got this ledger, I also bought some Speedball lettering pens and India ink and I began experimenting with calligraphy, which, as you can see here and on the next page, was still quite amateurish some three months later when Chrissie and I had just moved back to the commune. The ledger was the inspiration for my Straight Arrow collection of the same name. The two *Records* were really the roots of the book you are reading.

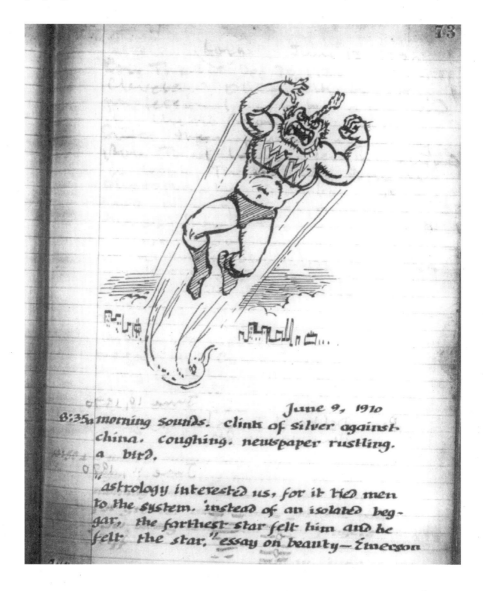

WONDER WART HOG
By Gilbert Shelton

Original ink drawing 12 cm. by 14 cm. in Jules Siegel's *Record* ledger
June 6, 1970, The Chinese House, Lagunitas, Calif.

know better than to hear something and then plaster the doors of Broadway with this info, trying to draw the Guinea Worm out of its lair. I personally find it fascinating. To be fair, we are being given an opportunity to find out about the habits and character of one of the major literary artists of this century—and such curiosity has only been fueled by his reclusiveness. (Alas, perhaps, but look at the time in which we live. This kind of stuff, I'm afraid, is a part of us now. One cannot deny one's date.)

And I sense very little bitterness or hostility coming from Jules and/or Chrissie. In fact, I'm surprised by the very lack of such negative energy.

Steven Maas <maas@cutr.eng.usf.edu> wrote

JULES SIEGEL WROTE: *I am also unimpressed by much of what passes as "academic" literature and "fine" art. I think performance art and installation art are mostly doper hoaxes. I'm into hyper-realism and traditional typography."*

Just because Pynchon is read and studied by academics does not make his work "academic." The academics on this list may disagree, but they have no more "claim" to Pynchon's work than do others. The thing I've never been able to figure out is why so many people want to take a book (*Gravity's Rainbow*) that's so much fun to read and turn it into work! Talk about yer Puritan heritage. As for clarity and accessibility, much of *Gravity's Rainbow* is as clear and accessible as Dr. Suess. Sure there are passages that leave me wondering, but—just like mysterious customs encountered while visiting exotic lands—that's part of the fun.

---

tstanton@nationalgeographic.com wrote:

MASCARO WROTE: *I don't know if T. Stanton thinks he agrees with me or if he thinks he's correcting me, but I guess I wasn't clear in my post. I agree completely w/ what you say about drugs and the creative process. My point is, why mention it all, unless it is in some way to diminish the creative process, which is what I feel Siegal tries to do to P's work w/ repeated digressions into P's alleged drug use. I think that is very uncool.*

At the risk of offending Jules, I think he knows exactly what he's doing. I'm just not offended by his bringing it up because it *is* central to the author, the Puritanism, guilt, liberation, and so on. I am uncomfortable that there is a bit too much inside personal info, and agree with an earlier post that we have a chance to ask the loftier questions.

The most interesting & revealing thing Chrissie has disclosed is the comic panel technique. Not the coffee can, drugs, kookiness, etc. (but I do like MacThrifty Pynchon & the thread on royalties vs. survival—fun stuff).

We just may be having the first chance to explore a new form of unauthorized biography. Don't be too angry with Jules & Chrissie, but don't be too forgiving either. This is a guilty pleasure & so far everyone is culpable.

—Tom Stanton

---

davemarc@panix.com wrote:

Since folks who feel a bit guilty about hearing (alleged) personal details about P. have let themselves be heard, I guess I'll just stick my e-neck out and state that I don't see anything terribly offensive or invasive about any of the "revelations" posted thus far—and I doubt that I will feel guilty about reading any subsequent postings. Maybe I've grown insensitive from reading too many issues of *People*, or from obsessively watching television talk shows, or maybe I'm just as interested in biography as I am in literature, but that's how I feel.

I'm sure that Jules and Chrissie will heed the following kind of advice, from Arlene Rinaldi's Netiquette Guide: "Never send or keep anything that you would mind seeing on the evening news."

Sorta salivating,

—davemarc

Diana York Blaine <dyb0001@jove.acs.unt.edu>

O.K., my turn. I, too, feel a tad tawdry over this interview business, like we're picking over someone's corpse but from a long way away and much later and we're having to use someone else's hands to do it. Also, as an academic (I guess I'll just admit that now), I am uncertain of the degree to which the making the connection between human banalities (in this case Pynchon's) and literary creations (his amazing oeuvre) can illuminate or even correspond. And this from someone who has read *People* and the *Enquirer*.

Not that I attended the funeral of the death of the author despite Roland Barthes' invitation, but I have definitely enjoyed TRP's mysterious persona

precisely because it permits the literature to speak for itself.
And by the way, re: that crack about academics interpreting
things best left alone and *Gravity's Rainbow* being as accessible
as Dr. Suess, HOOEY. Would you care to explain *V.* to me, Miss
Maryann? I'm still trying to figure out what the hell or who
the hell that woman is and regressing to everything I learned
in kindergarten ain't going to help.

One last thing (I guess we can blame the pugilistic
Mascaro—I'm not usually this sarcastic—thanks John! I miss
ya!), I am wondering how old some of the people on this list
are. Do you really still get a good buzz when you smoke pot?
Good Lord, I quit having unadulterated fun while high at
least seventeen years ago. It didn't stop me from doing it for a
long time but the lasting effect was paranoia, (now there's a
connection to Pynchon, I'll grant ya) not insight and
groovitude. Love and Fall Colors!

Gardener Cady <cadyg@elwha.evergreen.edu> wrote:

Diana York Blaine wrote: *Do you really still get a good buzz
when you smoke pot?*

I have also been wondering about our age-span. I am currently in my second year of college (19 yrs old.), have been
reading GR since my last year in high school (and I am on
page 161, I think). I took a break to read *The Crying of Lot 49*
and other stuff. I still "get a good buzz"" (you mean that stops?),
speaking of "buzz," I just completed my third psilosybin experience, IT was amazing. I thought about Pynchon so
much, I kept thinking about the Pirate's banana breakfast, I
would have eaten a banana or ten if it weren't for the nausea.
I have read that Banana sequence about four hundred times, it
is delicious. Thanky T. Pynchon.

—G. Cady

Diana York Blaine wrote: 'Do you still really get a good buzz when you smoke pot?'

paul.murphy@utoronto.ca wrote:

I must admit to having been entertained by Jules and Chrissie's reminiscences. All the same, reading about TRP's teeth is like reading about Sam Beckett's boils or Shostakovich's love of football—arouses my curiosity, but doesn't exactly help me understand GR or *Comment C'est* or String Quartet No. 13.

My 2 Canadian pennies,

—Paul

JULES REPLIES: Pynchon himself felt that his teeth shaped his life. I will discuss this at greater length later. Suffice it to say, that psychoanalytically writing is an oral expression.

> *I meant to later mention the "Psychodontics" satire in* V. — *in which much is made of the connection between psychoanalysis and dentistry.*

MantaRay@aol.com wrote:

I feel fine about asking private questions and jerking off. Not a problem.

I do not necessarily see the point of all the poring we do over every page the man wrote, then turning the other way when we have the opportunity to get some concrete insights, for fear of shame or whatever. I am still thanking Jules and Chrissie every night before I go to bed for giving me the opportunity to ask some questions and have them answered. Plus, so far, the postings have been really funny.

And, hey, if TRP wants to "come down off his pedestal" and smoke a joint, I'll buy the pot! The Crumb comments were worth the price of a bag.

Peace

—Scott Thill
Berkeley, CA

Geirland@aol.com wrote:

Can you post the text of your Playboy *piece? The people on this list are screaming for it.*

JULES: Anyone who wishes to can scream my way and I will e-mail a copy. I haven't heard anything yet. I prefer to do it this way until I can sort out the copyright issues. I don't want it to pass into the public domain. Please don't re-copy it or post it anywhere.

I have a rather prosaic question about Pynchon. How did he support himself in the years prior to the publication of Gravity's Rainbow? *I can't imagine that* V. *or* The Crying of Lot 49 *or the stories earned him enough to support him during the first 15 years of his career.*

He was always quite frugal. I believe all of his books have been reprinted many times in a number of languages. I think he would have been able to live adequately on his royalties.

Vaska Tumir <vaska@geocities.com> wrote:

I don't have the relevant stuff on or near me, but I remember some years ago looking into the number of editions and reprints of *V.* and *The Crying of Lot 49.* The figures were fairly staggering: if my memory serves me at all accurately, *V.* had had over 18 printing runs (in just one of the editions) well before 1973. Pynchon's reputation as a heavy-weight was pretty firmly established with the publication of *V.*, which brought him almost immediate international attention. I imagine that his royalties on the first two novels must have been adequate to substantial in 1960s terms.

Also (sorry to go on at this length), somebody asked Chrissie to identify some of the characters based on Pynchon's friends. I always thought that the Roger-Jessica-Jeremy triangle was a major piece of fictionalized autobiography on Pynchon's part, a hunch confirmed (for me, at least) when I read Jules' *Playboy* article sometime in the mid '80s. The same triangle-motif reappears in *Vineland,* another carry-over bit from *Gravity's Rainbow.*

Nice web-site, Jules.

<maas@cutr.eng.usf.edu> wrote:

Diana York Blaine wrote: ... *for itself. And by the way, re: that crack about academics interpreting things best left alone...*

Huh? What I said was "Just because Pynchon is read and studied by academics does not make his work academic." Nothing there telling litcrit types not to do your thang.

...and GR being as accessible as Dr. Suess, hooey.

To once again return to what my post actually said, it said that *much of* GR is as clear and accessible as Dr. Suess—a significantly different statement from what your misrepresentation would lead one to believe I said. What is this, a political ad?

Would you care to explain V. *to me, Miss Maryann? I'm still trying to...*

Wha??? Miss Maryann??
                              —Steve Maas

From: Jules Siegel <jsiegel@pdc.caribe.net.mx>
Subject: Hail Holy Light!

Good morning, world!

What a great day here in Cancun! We had a big storm yesterday and today everything is washed clean and hanging out to dry, smiling and nodding in the breeze. Lots of migrating birds beginning to show up, too. The lagoon is royal purple, the sky a misty blue with lots of pale cotton-puff clouds. When I hear the word culture, I reach for my bathing suit.

Can we have a show of hands here:

I thought people might like to see what Chrissie looked like when this was all going on. I have a couple of exquisite pictures taken of her at the commune after Faera was born by Ron Thal, then one of *Playboy*'s top photographers. No, Chrissie is not nude, although there are a whole bunch of others of naked lads and ladies being free to be me.

Post? Don't post?

I sent the article as an attachment, instead of putting the code in the body of the message.

Care? Not care?

I would also like to begin posting in HTML, as some of these things are getting a bit complex and will be easier to read and understand on-screen if I can use full editorial style including subheads and so on.

Yes? No?

Chrissie gave me a little blue velvet neck pillow with this embroidered slogan: "Don't worry. Be crabby!" She's a Cancer with Moon in Scorpio, Leo rising. When we lived in the commune, she embroidered Cancer symbols on all my shirts. Girls would ask me, "Are you a Cancer?" No, Libra. "So why the Cancer symbol?" My wife put it there. Very effective. Neither of us wore wedding rings, but I might as well have been branded. I probably should have lied, but lying is against my code. Cheating wasn't. It is now. To cheat without lying is merely a technical problem, requiring some quick thinking.

The computer that I am typing this on was a gift from her husband, Bob Wexler. When they visit Faera, they always bring lavish gifts for all of us—even for Anita. This time Robert bought me a new modem and 16 MB of RAM. Anita's mother was visiting, too, as well as Mary and Amy, two of Chrissie's friends. On my 61st birthday, Oct. 21, Robert took all of us to lunch in the hotel's palm-thatched beachfront restaurant. The birthday cake was chocolate truffle and the kids were wearing the new clothing that Robert and Chrissie and Anita's mother had brought them. *Omnia vincit amor.*

Hail holy light, creator of all that is!

Agree? Disagree?

> *The answers to my questions: yes, post picture; yes, prefer text of article as ascii in body of message; no, html code.*

Ted Samsel <tejas@infi.net> wrote:

JULES WROTE: *When I hear the word culture, I reach for my bathing suit.*

What? No *Montejo Leon*?

JULES REPLIES: *Dos Equis Oscuro,* but never at dawn. *León Negro* is another favorite. We start the day here with a full cup of coffee from Coatepec, Veracruz, or

Oaxaca *Pluma*—made in an espresso machine and heavily laced with sugar and cream. This morning my beautiful wife mixed both varieties.

Dynamite. Her too. More really.

---

clark@shepfs2.und.ac.za wrote:

Dear Jules,

I've been enjoying your comments on pynchon-l@waste.org, but this is too much... here in Durban on the Indian ocean coast it's cold, wet and raining, and the coffee is shit (though the woman with whom I'm sharing a flat isn't). Carry on describing paradise like this and I may end up hating you... :-)

—Craig Clark

> "Living inside the system is like driving across the countryside in a bus driven by a maniac bent on suicide."
>
> —Thomas Pynchon, *Gravity's Rainbow*

The little smiley face after "hating you...." is called an emoticon—from "emotions" and "icon." It's there to make sure that everyone understands that this is a joke. Because of the lack of visual cues, e-mail can intensify minor quips into vicious insults, so folks use these little figures as the textual equivalent of the raised eyebrow. There's even one that actually does look like a raised eyebrow. I personally hate emoticons and rigorously edit them out of all texts, so this is the last one you'll see here.

Part 4:
What did Lolita Say
About Humbert?

Preliminary Note: This is the transcript of my second session with Chrissie, which took place in my home beginning at about 8:30 pm, Monday, October 28, and ending at about 10:30 PM. In order to keep things better organized than the last session, which took place at her hotel, I had prepared all the questions in a single document and written my own answers earlier in the day. She came over with Robert and Faera, with a shopping bag of more new clothing for Eli and Jesse, but they were an hour late because there was an accident on the road and traffic was jammed up. They will be leaving Cancun tomorrow at 1 PM. She was in a terrible mood and it was hard to get her going.

> *"How about how irritable you were as a result of having to wait?"*
> *—Anita.*

Eli had set up the cassette recorder earlier, which had been working perfectly, but after a few minutes Chrissie said crankily, "I don't want to be on tape," and I stopped the recorder. We tried to play back the little bit we had recorded and the tape just made a grumbling noise.

Robert and Anita and Faera and the kids picked up the hint and disappeared into other rooms while Chrissie and I sat out in the living room and she scowled at me. I read off the questions and then entered her answers into a portable computer. I verified her direct answers by reading them back to her. There was a lot of hostile digression which I did not transcribe. Basically, I pretty much wished I had never been born. The kids were peeping in and out and choking back giggles. Faera and Anita and Robert snickered loudly during certain non-academic exchanges. I thought about what a Colombian friend said to me after coming back from seeing his ex-wife there: *"La realidad quita mucha la nostalgia."* Reality sure eliminates nostalgia. Where I paraphrase her answers, it's because there was too much going on to sit there just typing.

Following are the questions that got answered in one form or another.

Brad Schreiber <aro73@lafn.org> wrote:

Was Pynchon a night owl? Did he, like myself, get very upset by extraneous noise? Chrissie, when you were with him, did you sometimes get the feeling he was "brainstorming by himself," rather than being truly present in your company?

CHRISSIE: All of the above.

I once had a writing teacher tell me that writers often talk the way they write: verbose, taut, florid, etc. Is this true for TRP? Was he prone to flights of eloquence, leaving those in his company wondering when in blazing hell they would squeeze a word in edgewise?

CHRISSIE: That's him. He was constantly talking. He talked a lot about the prices of things. *[L. L. Bean down east voice:]* "Well, steak has gone up another fifty cents a pound—inflation, that's what it is. Have you noticed the price of dishwashing detergent?" He was like a little old lady. He talked on the phone for hours with Candida Donadio, his agent. He liked to talk about how paranoid he was.

Brett Coley <bcoley@vnet.ibm.com> wrote:

Is he a neat-freak, slob, or somewhere in between?

CHRISSIE: He was normal, dusty and neat, a bachelor. He never had a maid. He was very upset by people cleaning his windshield. He felt people should clean their own windshields. It was almost as if they were acting like servants. What kind of decent person would have a slave doing their windshields? It would be beneath your sense of decency and fair play. He didn't actually say all these words, but it was his body language, the sense of drama, the injustice of it all. Something as silly as that would provoke this dramatic response.

He was very down to earth. It was almost quaint—trying to be one of the proletariat, saving scraps of paper, saving everything. He always did the dishes and helped out, very, very sincere. The neighbors used to bring their children over for him to baby sit. They always knew that in a pinch Tom would baby sit. He was such a good solid citizen, nothing like you'd think a novelist would be, not very dashing.

The only colors he wore were dark military green and tan, generic clothes, and they were always baggy and kind of falling off. He had a woman friend down the street, a very intellectual rich woman married to a doctor, and she used to give him her husband's old shoes and clothing.

James F. Bisso <jbisso@us.oracle.com > wrote:

What lead Pynchon to join the Navy as an enlisted man. It doesn't seem like anything the scion of an old aristocratic family should do.

JULES: I think it would have been part of his attempt to escape his heritage and achieve oneness with the common man. He was quite proud about having worked with road crew when his father was a public official in Oyster Bay. Also, the educational benefits were excellent and he was hardly ROTC material. Other than that, I don't know, maybe he liked the adorable uniform.

The Pynchons were not aristocrats in the usual sense, though. I don't know to what extent the heritage really mattered to him on a conscious level. They weren't Old Money, but Old Family without money. This is a really difficult position to be in, as Chrissie has so eloquently laid out for us. I was impressed by the Colonial portraits and the 18th Century house because I was a simple Jewish boy from The Bronx. Despite what Chrissie says, he might have considered them merely old paintings and the house just an old house. It was quite austere and rather small, hardly palatial.

Bilge Ebiri <ebiri1@aol.com> wrote:

Did you ever get any sense of any events/places/times in TRP's life that seemed to have shaped him or his writing, or even, his deciding to write? Did he ever talk about such things? For example, his stint in the Navy?

CHRISSIE: No, no [very impatiently], he never talked about things like that. He never talked about the Navy. What did he care about the Navy? It was just some stupid thing he did because he probably didn't know what to do next. Are these really questions that people sent in? This is why he doesn't want to do interviews. Who are these people? A bunch of academic powder butts?

CHRISSIE
The Chinese House
Lagunitas, Calif., August, 1969
Photograph by Ron Thal

JULES: I believe he served on a minesweeper or a destroyer. He once told me that you could only understand the Navy by living on one of these ships—the confinement, dreariness, boredom.

How much research does he do?

JULES: I know that he did a lot of research, but I'm not sure that it was always focused on something he was writing, but more like something he happened to be fascinated by that he would then work into some current project.

Scott Thill <mantaray@aol.com> wrote:

Does TP ever express admiration or its opposite of some of his contemporary writers? What does he feel about the state of literature? Does he ever mention any other writers, like Don DeLillo, who many scholars, including myself, are sort of lumping him together, for better or worse, with?

CHRISSIE: They were always sending him books to read, which he read religiously. He said that he wished he could just write plainly like Jules. I think he thought he was too wordy. He always complimented the writer even if he hated him.

He liked to talk about Mimi Baez and Richard Fariña. He had a big affair with Mimi Baez. He told me all about it. He said Mimi and Richard were living in a cabin in the woods while Richard was writing his book. They were so poor that all they were eating was lentils and they were suffering from malnutrition and that Fariña couldn't ever eat lentil soup again.

Then when both their books came out, Pynchon got mad when they put him in the same category as Richard Fariña—same quality writing, same subject matter, those wild and crazy hipsters, what'll they think of next?

He wanted *The Crying of Lot 49* to be heavy and about pain and alienation. He didn't want it to be wild and wacky. He didn't see it that way. He saw it as a black and white movie and they saw it as tangerine-colored psychedelic pop music. They humiliated him. And then to top it off, it was on the same level as Richard Fariña!

He loved Nabokov. He was just like Humbert Humbert in *Lolita*. He had a big thing for Lolitas. That's why he went for me. But he liked hanging out with older women. There was no male bonding. He just didn't choose to do it. He thought they were intellectually superior to his contemporaries. He was capable of turning on the male act. He would have made a great actor. He was capable of fooling anyone. He had a friend who was a stupid surfer guy and he pretended he was on his level. He could slip into any character he wanted. He was really crafty, methodical. He was spying on people a lot of time, just observing. He liked to look in people's bookcases to find junky books to read.

JULES: He commented favorably on John Speicher, author of *Looking for Baby Paradise*, for which he wrote a puff in 1966 or '67. I believe he said, "This Speicher cat can really write!" Tom's use of doper slang always reminded me of jazz behind the Iron Curtain during the Cold War. Hop? Hep? Hip!

He also liked Jorge Luis Borges, whose "blurry Argentine Spanish" he mentioned he was reading in a letter to me from Mexico in 1964. I've never tried reading him in Spanish, but Borges is one of my favorite writers, easily the most important influence in my own writing. You always know exactly where you are in one of his stories—and he takes you to what at first appear to be some very strange spaces, but then you realize you have been there before on your own.

Juan Cires Martinez <jcm@mat.upm.es> wrote:

What correspondences do you see between specific real people and characters of his. For example, which character(s) is(are) based on you? On other people we might know?

JULES: Chrissie didn't want to talk about this and got quite annoyed when I brought it up. "This all happened thirty years ago! I was 19!" she exclaimed. "I've talked to him maybe five times for five minutes each since then! Why are you giving him all this free publicity, anyway!" She said she never said anything at all to me about him as a lover and that I made up that paragraph in my article. I told her that I had paraphrased what she said and that I put it there because I was trying to be nice to him. She didn't want me to be nice to him. I made her look like an imbecile.

I had to point out to her that I made her read the article line for line before I submitted it because I didn't want any problems later with *Playboy* and that she was happy with it and told me to send it in. She retorted that this was impossible. The article was published when she was living on Kauai with Gary. What did she ever get out of it anyway? I reminded her that I wrote the piece in 1975, when we were living in the Ford House in Mendocino but that *Playboy* took two years to publish it. I used the extra $1,000 that Arthur sent me when it came out to buy round-trip tickets for Faera and her to come back from Hawaii. I reminded her that she cashed the ticket in and brought Gary back too.

We were now marching around the room shouting at each other and she yelled at me, "Everyone cares about his privacy. Has anyone expressed any concern about my privacy, about your privacy? Do you know he was a fucking anti-Semite? Should I tell them all the shitty things he used to say about the Jews? You're just going to typecast me here like everyone does. Oh, little Shirley Temple, the stupid little thing. Everyone picks up on that, right?"

I tried to get her back to the question. She said there was a scene in one of his books in which a character tells a lover that she had thickened since having a baby by his rival, but that she could always come to him, baby and all. She felt that this was based on a photograph of her with Faera as a newborn by Ron Thal that appeared in my collection, *Record*. She was so angry, however, that it was not clear whether she was just talking about a scene in a book, or if something like this had also happened between them.

She went into another prolonged complaint about how all I ever did was make her look stupid in everything I wrote about her. Finally, I got really mad and just told her to shut the fuck up and go back to her hotel and just get out of my life forever. I turned off the computer and started to walk out of the room, but thought better of it, as I could hear muffled laughter all around. Dogs were barking frantically as if imitating us. She pulled in her horns a little and we split a *Dos Equis*. I turned the computer back on and read out loud the description of her below that I had written earlier today. Her mood changed considerably, and she laughed excitedly when I came to the part about the Ingmar Bergman movie, but she was still extremely out of sorts.

Bianca, obviously, is based on Chrissie, who matured very late physically. The first time Tom met her, she still had a thin wire orthodontic retainer. She thought it quite funny to play this effect deadpan to the max, especially with strangers, who sometimes failed to get the joke. It was also a defense mechanism, of which she was very aware. She was street smart, way ahead of people. In my article, I talk about her Shirley Temple imitations. Chrissie was the world's greatest dancer. She won first prize in a dance contest in one of those big teen dance halls in Manhattan Beach. She was there at the peak of the ecstasies in the Haight and the Summer of Love. They danced like Hasidim, only it was all naked sex, but *holy*. Man, did she dance. You saw the White Goddess in hot flesh and teenage underwear when Chrissie danced.

She had a beautiful singing voice, but it was small, like her, otherwise she might have been a top performer, except for her contempt for anything that wasn't literature or art, and I mean Art. We went to see *El Topo*, because I was doing a story on Alejandro Jodorowski. Well, you guys know me by now. Mystified. Yawning. She is sitting there in rapt concentration, a very icon of the cliché. Afterward she sums up the movie for me in, like, six sentences. I said, "I wish you could have told me that before we went in." So you can see how she and Tom would have been real tight.

I also feel very strongly that she had an influence on Tom's writing style, in the sense of bringing out his visual scene-setting skills, which I remember as being notably absent from *V.*, except in moments like the clock eye and the cheval glass and some of the scenes in German West Africa. I imagine the more concrete visual style that I perceived in what I read of *Gravity's Rainbow* was mostly the result of his maturing as a writer, but I suspect that she had an important influence.

The only way I can help you on this is to tell you how she influenced me. Chrissie is a brilliant watercolorist, but she hardly ever paints. She corrected my watercolor technique and she also taught me to recognize the importance of my visual environment, to see the meaning of things as gestalts. We were at Brian Wilson's one night and Brian said, "Look at Louie on the rug." It was a rich brown Weimaraner on a violet rug. Afterward, she said, "He was communicating his ecstasy. He gets so high, he can't really speak, and so he points with his voice to the vision of the dog on the rug."

Chrissie was always an absolute telepath. She could just appear in my brain. I would be sitting somewhere reading and feel her presence in my mind and then look around and see her as if painted on the wall like a fresco, only she was standing there and had been for a while, watching me read. Chrissie used words as captions under telepathic pictures that she projected directly into your mind. You became aware of how the light fell on a person's face, and that this had a Meaning.

It was like hanging out with Irwin Panofsky and Ansel Adams, only a lot better, because it was this unbelievably beautiful little blonde girl with huge green eyes and eyelashes like a moth's wings, a perfect figure like one of the water nymphs in the Blue Danube sequence of *Fantasia*, wearing a skimpy ecru cotton-knit shift and no underwear at all, an over-sized blue man's fedora and Tom Sawyer schoolboy oxfords for girls from the children's shoe department at Saks Fifth Avenue. Maybe she'd have on yellowing old welfare spectacles without lenses, because she was being Miss Jolly, your favorite art appreciation teacher.

When I went to the movies or to a museum with her I saw things in a way I never had before. Once we went with Tom Nolan to see Ingmar Bergman's "Hour of the Wolf." We were in the required state of the time to see a movie. It was always a problem to figure out how to get out of the house. You know, you had to get up and cross the room, open the door, very complex actions. Then there were the street lights. Magnificent street lights. Just stay right there and examine the workmanship of the street lights. Why go to a movie?

Anyway, I saw the movie through her eyes. It wasn't mysterious at all. It made perfect sense. It was a comedy. We knew all these people. Bergman was satirizing them all, even the poor pregnant wife. When the crazy writer (or artist, or whatever he was) shows his drawing and says ominously, "Here is the lady who takes off her face," we had absolute hysterics, roaring with laughter, as Nolan cringed down in his seat and tried to pretend he wasn't with us and people starting angrily shushing us. The characters in the film were the kind of nutballs we dealt with at the commune. We were crazy, but, gee, we weren't frightened all the time, constantly putting everyone on attention-getting trips by being worried about the walls turning into cake icing, or whatever.

Sometimes people have very crucial influences on each other. They don't have to be together for a long time to learn a lot from each other. I feel very strongly that Chrissie broke Tom out of his shell, at least while she was with him. You would have to see a picture of her at the time to understand what she would have meant to him. People not only used to stop and stare at her on the street, but also comment to each other in loud, astounded voices. I think she got into his head and walked around in there and rearranged the furniture. This is more important than Bianca as a character. So it was an explosive combination.

Gardener Cady <cadyg@elwha.evergreen.edu> wrote:

Does he like TV and junk food?

CHRISSIE: He loved junk food, but he wasn't fussy; he would just eat anything. He used to eat pizza to comfort himself. Once after taking me home to Jules mother's place in Beverly Hills, he was upset about our relationship and so he stopped for a slice of pizza to comfort himself, and while he was eating the pizza, someone was climbing in the window of his apartment and stealing his stereo. He blamed this on me. I was a jinx. I brought bad luck into his life. Couldn't see me any more. That was a joke, by the way. That was his sense of humor. I wasn't supposed to take that seriously.

Another time, he said "Let's go see Jules and confront him and tell him that we want to live together." I had some ambivalent feelings about that *[laughs sardonically]*. We had to stop and have a pizza to calm his stomach. He was a little too shy around other people. I was shy, too. I didn't think that was a good idea. I'd never get to meet anybody.

He broke up more than one marriage, because he was too shy to find someone on his own. He made friends with couples and went off with the wife. He felt that men in general are impressed with women that other men have approved of, that there was an added attraction as a result of this.

What bothered me about him is that he didn't seem as if he were very brave. He was cautious. I hate that. He was not a daredevil, believe me. You could never picture Thomas Pynchon on the high wire in the circus. *[More very loud sardonic laughter.]*

Craig Clark <clark@shepfs2.und.ac.za> wrote:

Pynchon seems considerably interested in Namibian history. It is a major theme in both V. *and* Gravity's Rainbow. *As a South African who visited Namibia while it was still illegally occupied by my home country, I wondered, has Thomas Pynchon visited Namibia?*

CHRISSIE: He'd never have gone to Africa. It would have been too much of an adventure.

She got up and said, "This is enough of this. Look, Jules, just send me a fax, and I'll answer the questions in writing." By now the others were getting tired of hiding out and everyone came out into the living room. "I'll send you a five-

CHRISSIE & FAERA
The Chinese House, Lagunitas, Calif., June, 1971
Photograph by Ron Thal

page letter," Chrissie said comfortingly, as they got ready to go. "I'm sure you will," I replied. "I'll call you on the telephone," she said. Robert and Faera were kind of hustling her out the door and laughing at us. "I'll put her on the Internet with you when we get back to the States," Robert said jovially, and we all said good-bye. Anita went into the bedroom to go to sleep and I stayed out here editing this into the shape you have it now.

No more questions for Chrissie, gang.

Well, maybe if someone is willing to pay me to do this again. I'll take Thorazine first.

Let's just get back to polymorphic semiotics and syncretism and heteronomy and all. I love academics. I am an academic. I live in an ivory tower and I am lucky. It's all academic anyway, as I am going to go to bed.

Whew. Just like old times. And to think how depressed I was when she left me. Do you think that Mick Jagger wants to go back and interview Maryanne Faithfull? Trust me when I tell you that Anita Brown is a lot cuter than Uma Thurman and Jerry Hall combined, too. Heteronomy. This is just another term that women have made up to keep men under control. Ron Thal once said, "They talk about being pussy-whipped. I say, hey, *whip* me with it!"

Anita opens the bedroom door and sticks in her head and half her naked body, blinking in the light and frowning, all blonde curls and tawny skin, "Don't you want to turn that light off and come in for now?" The door closes as she slips back into the darkness. I hit Ctrl-S and Exit yawning.

Part 5: Flame Wars

From: Diana York Blaine <dyb0001@jove.acs.unt.edu>
Subject: Jittery Jules

"some people claim that there's a woman to blame…"

From: Jules Siegel <mail.caribe.net.mx>
Re: Thanks to all

ckaratnytsky@nypl.org wrote:

Dear Guilty in DC, Just wanted to let you know that I was glad to read your recent comments re the online interview with Chrissie. I share your feelings. I have been concerned that I have been giving in to my baser instincts by reading the interview—and I disagree, btw, with Jules that this is like feeling guilty about jerking off. For me, it's a matter of not liking the fact that I've done some thing that I know is unkind or unpleasant or distasteful to someone who has made their feelings/wishes about it clear. Not feelin' holier than thou here, just a bit regretful… Guilty in NY, Chris

Dear Chris (and all),

I haven't looked at all my mail yet this morning, so I don't know what the reaction was to "Humbert & Lolita," but one reason Chrissie was so mad is that she feels that Tom exploited her and ridiculed her in *Gravity's Rainbow*. She had no idea he was going to write about her (and me, I guess, although I never looked for myself) in this way (and others that I haven't bothered to look into). She never got anything for it. Neither did I, and he had the nerve even to use my name in one of his stories. I was wondering if this insight causes you to change your opinion in any way about this issue. "Do unto others.…" So he's a great artist and that gives him certain prerogatives. Some people (Chrissie among them) feel I'm a great artist too. What gives here?

More importantly, Faera is going to be in New York next week. We really are desperate for books, so if your offer to help out on this is still open, can she look you up when she gets there? Any special place or time? I don't know if you were on the Pynchon article posting list, so I'm repeating below the advice about this I had there.

Maybe others who have books they'd like to contribute can coordinate with you, as the mails to Cancun are really slow.

I am under strict instructions from the $uperego $quad here to get back to work and stop fooling around online. If you really need to hear from me, please put "Jules, reply" in the subject line, as I am going to try not even to look into my mail for a few days. I'm sure that there's a more elegant way to do this, but I don't know what it is.

Meanwhile, my heartfelt thanks to all of you (especially to John Mascaro, who provoked what I felt was the high point of our exchange here, "A Midnight Visit With the Werewolf") for allowing me to be a guest and for your always thought-provoking reactions to my comments. I am going to see if I can get Chrissie to tell us more via Robert's offer to put her online, but I'm sure that you can all understand that this was a highly emotionally-charged experience for her and she needs some time to absorb it all.

From: Jules Siegel <jsiegel@pdc.caribe.net.mx>
Subject: Pynchon article

Dear Friends,

It's raining e-mail! I have just spent pretty much of a whole afternoon trying to answer all this great mail. It turns out to be too big a task to send the article out one by one, so I am posting it to the list.

Early next week it will also be on my website at:

http://www.caribe.net.mx/siegel/pynchon.htm

Who Is Thomas Pynchon...
And Why Is He Taking Off
With My Wife?

Shedding a little light on the most famous
author-recluse since j. d. salinger

memoir BY JULES SIEGEL

THOMAS RUGGLES PYNCHON, JR., is the most famous invisible writer since J. D. Salinger, the most admired since B. Traven, the most difficult since James Joyce. When his first novel, *V.*, was greeted with thundering critical applause in 1963, *Time* sent a photographer to find him in Mexico City. Pynchon fled to Guanajuato, then an eight-hour bus ride into the mountains, and has eluded all subsequent attempts to get his picture. In 1974, *New York* magazine scored a mini-coup by publishing a photo taken of him while he was in college.

Pynchon did not show up at the 1974 National Book Awards luncheon to receive his prize for his third novel, *Gravity's Rainbow*, co-winner in the fiction category with Isaac Bashevis Singer's *A Crown of Feathers*. His publisher sent, in his stead, double-talking comedian Irwin Corey, who bills himself as "the world's greatest expert on everything" and who accepted the prize with what *New York Times* reporter Steven R. Weisman described as "a series of bad jokes and mangled syntax that left some people roaring with laughter and others perplexed."

Weisman speculated that this was "evidently intended to make fun of the fact that the Pynchon novel, while hailed as a work of genius, also left many of its readers confused and baffled by its encyclopedic references and intricate, fantastic style."

Confused though the literary world may be by the mysterious Pynchon and his labyrinthine allegories, he has received unprecedented acclaim. *V.* won the William Faulkner Prize. His second novel, *The Crying of Lot 49*, took the Rosenthal Award in 1967. *Gravity's Rainbow* was the unanimous nomination of

ORIGINALLY PUBLISHED IN *Playboy*, MARCH, 1977

the Pulitzer fiction jury in 1974, but the advisory board of eminent journalists disagreed, calling the book "obscene," "unreadable" and "overwritten." The trustees skipped the prize entirely that year.

In 1975, Pynchon declined the William Dean Howells Medal of the American Academy of Arts and Letters, given every five years for a distinguished work of fiction, breaking silence with a brief note saying he knew he ought to accept the gold medal as a hedge against inflation, but no, thanks, anyway. The academy said it would hold it for him in case he changed his mind.

Although he has never had a best seller, Pynchon's books have been commercially successful. There are more than half a million copies of *V.* in print. Somewhere back of that pile of paper and ink there is a question mark named Thomas Pynchon, location unknown, of no fixed address, his biography a mere few sentences, physical description unavailable. Who is Thomas Pynchon, really? Why is he hiding? Does he exist at all, or is he no more than an elaborate hoax of the Age of Paranoia, like the hallucinatory inventions of Argentina's blind fabulist, Jorge Luis Borges? Who is Thomas Pynchon and what does he mean?

Everyone has his own fantasy of success. I once had no greater hope than to publish a learned paper on 17th Century English songs in *The Publications of the Modern Language Association*. Somewhere in the blank fog of time there is a scholar writing a learned paper on Thomas Pynchon. To him I offer this footnote: In "Mortality and Mercy in Vienna," Pynchon's first published short story, the protagonist is one Cleanth Siegel. My second wife, the former Virginia Christine Jolly of San Marino, California, tells me that the character represents me. I have noticed the coincidence of name but do not recognize myself. Possibly it is a me I have never been able to examine very well, the back of my neck, or the dream of Gabriel García Márquez, whose essential quality is that it cannot be remembered.

Be that as it may, I did attend Cornell in 1954. The boy in the next room was Thomas Ruggles Pynchon, Jr. If there are any correspondences to be found in that or anything else that follows, I leave them to Chrissie and the scholars.

Tom Pynchon was quiet and neat and did his homework faithfully. He went to Mass and confessed, though to what would be a mystery. He got $25 a week spending money and managed it perfectly, did not cut class and always got grades in the high 90s. He was disappointed not to have been pledged to a fraternity, but he lacked the crude sociability required for that. Besides, he had his own room at Cascadilla, one of the more pleasant dormitories, not tight College Tudor tile but pre-Civil War Victorian, high-ceilinged and muted. Fraternity houses offered neither the charm nor the privacy, and he was, if anything, a very private person.

Pynchon was then already writing short stories and poems, but he did not hand them about very much. I remember one story that had something to do with a broken pitcher of beer. I once saw some French quatrains in what looked like his hand—small, regular, precise engineer's manuscript. He later denied ever having done anything like that. Maybe they were a girl's, but I never met her, as far as I know.

I have seen photographs of William Faulkner that made me think of Tom. He was very tall—at least 6′2″—and thin but not skinny, with a pale face, fair eyes and a long, chiseled Anglo nose. He was ashamed of his teeth and did not smile much. Many years later, writing to me from Mexico City, where he was having extensive and painful dental restoration done, he described them as "misshapen choppers" and said they had determined his life in some unspecified way that seemed very important to him.

His wit was terrifically bold for such an otherwise cautious personality. He could carry a tune well and made up ribald parodies of popular songs, which I seem to remember—surely I am imagining this—were accompanied on a ukulele. From the musical notations in the back of T. S. Eliot's *The Cocktail Party*, he puzzled out for me the tune of "One-Eyed Reilly," which we sang together one beer-soaked night in joyous disharmony and stole an old wooden rocking chair off someone's porch and tossed it into the interior court of Cascadilla Hall. It landed upright on the roof of a covered crosswalk and rocked itself quiet. Possibly it is still there.

When his parents came to visit, he introduced his mother this way: "Jules, this is my mother. She's an anti-Semite." Susan Gordon later told me that when the remark was repeated to Mrs. Pynchon she replied, "I'm not an anti-Semite. I just didn't want my children to surround themselves with Jews." I remember her as an exceptionally beautiful woman, all cut glass, ivory and sable. I believe she had been a nurse, had a lot of Irish in her and was a Catholic. Though Mr. Pynchon was a Protestant, she raised their children in her own faith. Tom was the oldest. Then came Judith, about five years younger. The youngest was John.

I had more contact over the years with Mr. Pynchon than with Tom's mother, but he is less clear: curly, lightish hair, red nose, very friendly and tolerant. He was commissioner of roads for the town of Oyster Bay, Long Island, and Tom worked with the road crews in the summer. Mr. Pynchon later became supervisor of the town of Oyster Bay and is now an industrial surveyor. The Pynchons lived in a very plain New England frame house on Walnut in East Norwich, its most notable furnishings some excellent Colonial portraits of ancient Pynchons.

IT IS AN OLD AMERICAN FAMILY, dating back to William Pynchon, one of the founders and principal citizens of Spring Weld, Massachusetts, who left England March 29, 1630, with John Winthrop's fleet, accompanied by his wife and three daughters. His son, John, seems to have come over later on a different ship. The Pynchons are prominent in New England historical literature. William and John were magistrates and military officers. Their court record has survived and has been published in a carefully annotated edition by Harvard University Press, with a frontispiece portrait of William Pynchon. There are Tom's eyes and a lot of his nose and shape of face.

William Pynchon is remembered for his role in the witch trials, in which he appears to have been a relatively moderate force, and for his highly controversial book *The Meritorious Price of Our Redemption*, a protest against the rigid Calvinistic theology of his time, evidently the first by an American author. It was officially censured by the General Court, which ordered a rebuttal written, summoned Pynchon to explain himself and directed the book burned by the executioner in the Boston market place. Soon afterward, William Pynchon returned to England, leaving John to supervise the family's substantial holdings in the New World. He died October 29, 1662, and was buried in the churchyard at Wraysbury.

Although John Pynchon was an important man in his own time, an increasing obscurity gathered about the name. The Pynchons were Tories during the Revolution but loyal citizens of the republic afterward. By the time Nathaniel Hawthorne wrote *The House of Seven Gables*, in which a Pynchon appears in a not very attractive characterization, it seems that the family was virtually unknown. To Hawthorne's surprise, however, surviving Pynchons vigorously protested. In a letter dated May 3, 1851, Hawthorne apologized and wrote that he thought no great damage had been done, "but since it appears otherwise to you, no better course occurs to me than to put this letter at your disposal, to be used in such manner as a proper regard your family honor may be thought to demand."

Of the fate of the Pynchon family fortune, not much is to be found. They were gentry in England and gentry here. In the first half of the present century, the Wall Street Firm of Pynchon & Co. went under with scant attention, except for the comment of a Morgan partner that "these ripe apples must fall." When I knew them, the Pynchons appeared to be in relatively modest circumstances but hardly in want.

Though there are some well-known and evidently quite prosperous Pynchons—notably, the original Thomas Ruggles Pynchon—to be found in the standard biographical dictionaries and encyclopedias, the two most illustrious are separated by more than 300 years, covering the entire history of the nation. Indeed, it is not pure hyperbole to suggest that, in some measure, William Pynchon of Springfield and Thomas Pynchon of modern literary fame define the spectrum of our intellectual history. The records of the Pynchon family are easily accessible to any competent researcher. Curiously enough, no commentator on the younger Pynchon's work seems to have made the connection with his ancestor.

How CLOSE WERE TOM AND I AT CORNELL? It is hard to say, really. We were friends, maybe at some points best friends, very much alike in some important ways. We were both writers, both science students—he in electrical engineering, I in premed—both quite solitary and shy. Like him, I had no luck on fraternity row. Unlike him, I was not diligent, was careless with money, attended class rarely, hardly got grades at all, much less high ones. One weekend between sessions, we hitchhiked from Ithaca to Ann Arbor, Michigan, where I wanted to see a girlfriend named Esther Schreier at the University of Michigan. If you think that name is dissonant, try Esther Chachkis, which is what she became when she married.

It was blinding cold. We crossed Canada at night. Ann Arbor was sodden with stale snow. Esther had the flu and was not in a very romantic mood, though pleased to see me. Tom refused a date for himself and spent the evening at the observatory. On the way back, we got stranded on the bridge between

Detroit and Ontario for about eight hours waiting for a ride, freezing outside between brief shelters in the relative warmth of the men's room until the guards took pity on us and invited us into their hut and got us a ride.

This time, we blasted across the barren winter reaches with a wild pair of couples in a sedan and a pickup truck who played tag with the two vehicles in the darkness before dawn at speed upwards of 80 mph, sometimes turning their headlights off to ensure surprise. One of us—I forget which—left his bag in the car when they let us off in Buffalo. Tom remembered the first name of one of the men and that he worked for cab company. We had to wait a couple of hours or more in a White Tower Hamburger stand until the cab companies' telephones were answered. Then we tracked them down and got the bag back. It took us most of the day to get back to Ithaca. Tom began talking with the Southern Colonel's accent, not only to me but also to everyone we met. Before long, I was pleading with him to stop.

Not long after that, I dropped out of school and went into the Army, winding up in the Military Intelligence service in Korea, where I received a letter from Pynchon informing me that he, too, had left school and now was—I laughed out loud at the piquant turn of speech—"a jolly jack-tar." He returned to Cornell, an English major this time, where Vera Nabokov thinks she remembers grading his papers for her husband's class. Of Vladimir Nabokov, Pynchon told me only that his Russian accent was so thick he could hardly understand what he was saying. I did not return to Cornell but went, instead, to Hunter College.

I saw Pynchon occasionally in New York. Once he took me down to Greenwich Village to the Cafe Bohemia, where Max Roach was playing. It was the only band I ever heard in which the drums carried the melody. The Modern Jazz Quartet and the Kent Micronite Filter commercial were about as much modern music as I could handle. Pynchon, however, was deeply into the mysteries of Thelonious Monk. On religious grounds, I excused myself from attending chapel with him at the Five Spot to hear "God" play. I was an atheist.

Tom came down to The Bronx to my engagement party, helped do the massive load of dishes and stayed overnight with us. In June 1958, Mr. Pynchon arranged for the marriage ceremony to be performed by a Federal district court judge in Massapequa, Long Island, and I went out to East Norwich to take care of the final details. His sister Judith was there, 16 and more than fair. I blushed with lust and wondered why I was getting married. When the appointed day came, we arrived at the judge's mansion to find his worship in a tuxedo. It seemed that a few days earlier, another young couple named Siegel had come to him and asked to be married. Thinking it was us, he had done so and crossed our name off his appointment calendar. Fortunately—is that the right word?—Tom arrived early and intercepted the judge, who was getting ready to go off to a formal dinner dressed in black tie. The marriage proceeded as planned. Phyllis DeBus became Mrs. Jules Siegel. Pictures were taken. In one of them, there was Tom, bearded, wearing a charcoal-gray suit. Perhaps Phyllis still has that picture. We were divorced less than four years later, our marriage a victim of deep family tragedies. I think of her occasionally with great affection and a certain longing. She was so wonderful a lover, generous and easily aroused, but I was too callow then to appreciate her.

Tom visited us when we were living in Queens, once helping us move from one apartment to another, playing a wastepaper basket as a conga drum in the back of the rented step van. Another time, he came down from Ithaca with his girlfriend, Ellen Landgraben, a coed at Cornell. It was a forbidden love. She was Jewish and her parents objected to Tom. It was my job to drive her out to Hewlett and pretend that I had brought her from school. At the last minute, I forgot to remove my shiny wedding band. I don't know if they noticed, though.

I remember another visit shortly after I was graduated from Hunter and was working for a public-relations agency. The firm was soliciting an account in the field of atomic research that manufactured plastic mannequins called radiation dummies, made of materials designed to absorb radiation in exactly the same way as the human body. One model had a human skeleton. The other was all plastic. Both had clear skins of something like Lucite and were eerily beautiful. I had the literature at home. Tom took some of it with him when he left. I was not to see him again for more than five years.

There were letters. Eventually, the total was something like thirty. They began from Seattle, where he worked on the Boeing company magazine. I remember one from Florida. He was then living with a girl and they had gone to visit her family. A cute preteen attracted Tom's notice enough for him to mention her lasciviously. Soon the letters had a Mexico City postmark. The Mexicans laughed at his mustache and called him Pancho Villa. In the rainy season, he awoke one morning to find a drowned rat on his balcony. Guanajuato was a town of stone corridors twisting back on one another. I had complained about the complexity of *V.* "Why should things be easy to understand?" he

retorted and followed with a brief dissertation on the origins of the simple
English movement in the studies of comprehensibility of newspaper copy commissioned by the Associated Press. The death of Marilyn Monroe grieved him
heavily. The girl was no longer with him. This letter was written with a brand-
new Mexican ribbon. He was gnashing his misshapen choppers in envy of my
corrosively elegant first drafts of short stories and letters complaining of my
inability to write. The return address changed, but the form of the letter was
always the same: neatly typed on engineer's quadrille paper, the signature in
faint pencil, "Tom."[2]

By 1965, he was living in Manhattan Beach, California. I had given up the
public-relations business and was free-lancing for magazines. *The Saturday Evening
Post* sent me to California to do a story on Bob Dylan. I found Tom in a one-
room apartment with a view of the sea. There were some shabby furnishings,
a large gas heater, a narrow cot, a few books—one, *Totempole,* by Sanford Friedman—little else; a monk's cell decorated by the Salvation Army. I told him
about the Dylan assignment. "You ought to do one on The Beach Boys," he
said. I pretended to ignore that. A year or so later, I was in Los Angeles again,
doing a story for the *Post* on The Beach Boys. He had forgotten his earlier
remark and was no longer especially interested in them. I took him to my
apartment in Laurel Canyon, got him royally loaded and made him lie down
on the floor with a speaker at each ear while I played Pet Sounds, their most
interesting and least popular record. It was not fashionable to take The Beach
Boys seriously.

"Ohhhhh," he sighed softly with stunned pleasure after the record was done.
"Now I understand why you are writing a story about them."

Another time, Chrissie was there. I had met her at a Beach Boys record
session. She was then a few months older than 18, still wearing a thin wire
brace on her big white teeth. Of Chrissie, it is necessary to post certain warn-

[2]A letter from Thomas Pynchon to Richard Fariña is being offered by Ken López,
Bookseller, for $15,000. López notes that the letter was written on graph paper. In one
of the typically suspicious notes on my memoir that have appeared elsewhere on the
Internet, this news was greeted as confirmation that I had "gotten something right."
Pynchon dedicated *Gravity's Rainbow* to Fariña, but I have no reason to doubt Chrissie's
earlier remarks about how he felt about Fariña's status as a writer. I would guess that it
was Fariña's status as an underground cult figure that Pynchon admired, in addition to
his personal feelings for his friend.

ings. It is easy to underestimate her intelligence, but it is a mistake. She is obviously too pretty to be serious, conventional wisdom would have you believe. In New York, she was offered a screen test by Carlo Ponti the first week we arrived. She turned him down, likewise a modeling contract with the Ford agency, beginning with a recruiting commercial for the Coast Guard. The lady is full of surprises that do not go with a Pepsodent smile, shy and expert in the arts of invisibility, detesting stereotyped response. Her beauty is a device used to deflect inquiry, like the bullfighter's cape. There is the kiss of the rose on the point of a sword. When Tom left, I took him down to his old green Corvair parked at the bottom of the hillside. "Don't worry about her," he said.

"What is that supposed to mean?" I asked

"I think you worry about her. Don't. She can take care of herself."

We spent several days together, the three of us. One night we all went up to Brian Wilson's Babylonian house in Bel-Air. Brian then had in his study an Arabian tent made of crimson and purple Persian brocade. It was like being inside the pillow of a shah. There was one light, fashioned from a parking meter. You had to put pennies in it to make it stay on. Brian brought in an oil lamp and tried to light it. The parking-meter light kept going out and Brian kept dropping the oil lamp and stumbling over it. Neither he nor Pynchon said anything to each other. Another night, we went to Studio A at Columbia Records, only to find our way barred by one of Brian's assistants, Michael Vosse, who explained that we couldn't come in anymore, because Chrissie was a witch and fucking with Brian's head so heavy by ESP that he couldn't work.

One afternoon, Chrissie and I drove out to Manhattan Beach to see Tom, taking along with us some grass we had scored at a be-in (remember be-ins?) in Griffith Park. Tom was then living in a two-room studio with kitchen that had evidently been converted from a garage. It was on a side street a couple of blocks up from the beach. The decoration was pretty much the same. A built-in bookcase had rows of piggy banks on each shelf and there was a collection of books and magazines about pigs. The kitchen cabinets contained not groceries but many empty Hills Brothers coffee cans in orderly array, as if displayed on supermarket shelves.

His desk sat next to a window in the small living room. It had a clutter of miscellaneous papers, letters from obscure publications pleading for articles, an Olivetti portable typewriter, a thick stack of that graph paper covered with his fine script—the draft of *Gravity's Rainbow*, which he was in the process of typing and rewriting. He felt that he had rushed through *The Crying of Lot 49* in order to get the money. He was taking no such chance with the new book, apparently having begun it soon after the publication of *V.*, interrupting it to write *The Crying of Lot 49*. Much of the draft was done in Mexico. "I was so fucked up while I was writing it," he said, "that now I go back over some of those sequences and I can't figure out what I could have meant."

On the desk, there was a rudimentary rocket made from one of those pencil-like erasers with coiled paper wrappers that you unzip to expose the rubber. It stood on a base twisted out of a paper clip. The wrapper had been pulled up into a cone from which a needle protruded. I touched the needle with the tip of my finger and it fell into the cone. Tom frowned, cursed and spent at least a half hour tickling the needle back out again. As soon as he got it right and leaned back, I pushed it back in again. He put his face in his hands and almost wept.

THE GRASS WAS SAID TO BE ACAPULCO GOLD. It was strong and beautiful. The day was misty soft—cloudy water-color weather. We drove down the coast past a couple of towns to see an abandoned baroque hotel, something out of Bergman, but with a grand tattered Colonial flavor. As twilight thickened and condensed into liquid darkness, we returned to Manhattan Beach in relentlessly gathering fog. At night, we went down to the beach. The fog was so dense that the streetlights on The Strand disappeared a few yards' walk toward the sea. Enveloped in opal-gray night we floated in and out of one another's view, dancing down to the water. Only the foaming edge of the waves was visible, and even that was perceived mostly as a blurred lapping sound. We were alone on the empty margin of existence, walking the scant line between nowhere and nothing.

Too stoned to risk driving back to Laurel Canyon in the grainy fog, Chrissie and I slept the night in Tom's dank bedroom while he made do on his studio couch in the living room. The head of the bed sat in a low notch of damp painted concrete formed by the floor of the room above. The room was a cave.

In the morning, there was sunshine. As we sat in the kitchen, Tom said, "Do you believe in ESP? Strange things keep happening to me. One day I was sitting in here and the side of my head came off, opening into Candida's office, which I have never seen. She was talking on the telephone. Later, I spoke to her about it and told her what her office looked like. I had it all exactly right.

"You know the w.a.s.t.e. horn in *The Crying of Lot 49?* The symbol of the secret message service? Every weirdo in the world is on my wave length. You cannot understand the kind of letters I get. Someone wrote to tell me that the very same horn was the symbol of a private mail system in medieval times. I checked it out at the library. It's true. But I made it up myself before the book was ever published, before I ever got that letter."

When Chrissie and I got back home, there was a message for me to call a number in New York. It was the publisher of a new magazine for young people. He wanted me to go East and be editor. We left soon afterward without seeing Tom again. Less than a year later, depressed and whipped, I went back again to Los Angeles. We stayed in the Ramada Inn on Sunset Strip. Pynchon came bouncing into our room with a pound of excellent grass, the kind they called ice pack, and a chunk of violent hash. He was wearing a black-velvet cape. There was a mysterious undertone to his enthusiasm.

"What are you always so afraid of?" I asked him. "Don't you understand that what you have written will get you out of almost anything you might get yourself into?"

There was no answer, but looking into his face, I could see his thought as plainly as if has spoken out loud.

"You think that it is what you have written that they will want to get you for," I said.

A few days later, on February 4, 1968, just before I was to leave for my brother's birthday party, which was to be held on a big boat moored off San Pedro (James Gould Cozzens fans, note well), I slipped and fell and broke my hip. Tom had been invited to the party and, in fact, did show up, striking an acquaintance with Susan, a friend of Chrissie's from San Marino. Susan has red hair and is breathtakingly beautiful, with the voluptuous body of a showgirl. Like Chrissie, she is much brighter than she looks, but if Chrissie plays the Dragon Lady, Susan plays Gracie Allen. The children of San Marino, one of the headquarters of The John Birch Society, are careful to avoid open displays of subversive intellect. Susan once came to the shattering realization while strolling on a concrete sidewalk that none of the squares was true, that, indeed, there were not true perfect squares to be found anywhere in reality. She was overcome by tears, then by nameless dread. A psychiatrist in San Marino diagnosed her a paranoid schizophrenic and prescribed shock treatment and apparently was going to administer it on the spot. Now really in hysterics, she called her father, who very sensibly countermanded the doctor's orders and calmed his child himself. Since then Susan has been very careful in guarding her emotions, to the point where she sometimes seems stupid and cold. It is a pose.

Evidently, Tom saw through her mask, for the two went off and lived together for a long time. They came to visit me in the hospital and later at home, too. The last evening they were there, Michael Vosse showed up. He had some tarry black *ganja,* which he said had been grown high in the mountains by natives who beat the plants with whips woven of silver thorns to make them produce more resin. We smoked the grass. It was indescribably intense. The pain of my broken hip expanded to fill the room. I found myself unable to stand Michael's presence in the room and, after much reflective delay, finally asked him to leave.[3] Alone with Chrissie and Susan and Tom, I felt some relief, but now the smell of the kitchen garbage bothered me. Tom volunteered to take it out. Chrissie went off to show him the way. Susan and I lay back, unable to move. The mood turned overwhelmingly sexual. I wanted to make love to Susan, but I couldn't speak, overcome by the feeling and the karmic implications, my thought racing toward certain inevitable conclusions. The door opened. It was Tom and Chrissie. A little while later, he and Susan left. I knew then that it would be a very long time, if ever, before I saw him again.

Do you believe in ESP? I believe in everything and nothing. There are certain moments when it is all clear. The future lies spread out against your skull in blazing agony. There is the meaning of paranoia: not insanity but truth, the end of all our precious privacies, not the dignity of confession but the crazed gibber of the drooling beast.

Chrissie and I went back to New York. My career went from modest turn to modest turn and, before long, *Playboy* sent me to do a story on hippie communes in California. She went on ahead of me while I stayed and finished a story on Herman Kahn that was purchased but never published. It was more

---

[3] Michael visited me in Los Angeles in 1977 and told me how hurt he had been by the publication of this remark, which he felt made him seem as if he were some kind of leper. I really didn't mean it that way. The grass was really strong and I was in a lot of pain, even though I was still taking codeine. I didn't feel the kind of intimacy with him that I had with the others and I wanted to be alone with Chrissie and Tom and Susan because the pain was too strong for me to expose to someone who was a stranger compared with them.

than a month before I was to see her again. I felt the drift of her voice as she wandered off the telephone one day. It was nearly her birthday. I went down to B. Altman and sent her an ounce of Le De Givenchy. The day before I left to join her, it came back in the mail.

When I finally did reach Chrissie in Berkeley, where I had an assignment from *The New York Times Sunday* Magazine to do a story on the Black Panther Convention of 1969, the drift was subtle but real. She was on her way somewhere else and there seemed to be nothing that I could do to moor her interest. It was the week of the first landing on the moon. How appropriate that it was July, month of Cancer, of her birthday. After the convention, we visited a commune out in the redwoods and lived there for something like a month. Then I went off to Taos with a photographer and had various experiences, prophetic dreams and insidious anxieties I will possibly detail in some other work. I saw very far and well and truly, made certain decisions and returned to my wife not afraid.

One day we went for a walk in the redwoods and I said, "Chrissie, I love you more than any woman I have ever known, as much as I love my own mother. Something is troubling you. I think that it will make you feel better if you tell me what it is."[4]

"I had an affair with Tom," she answered.

There it was. I felt all the things you feel in those circumstance, but mostly a sense of karma. Karma is what you get for what you do. It is also a certain perspective of reality. The words are flimsy, but the fact is about as graceful as a faceful of shit. Once, a long time ago, I had an affair with another man's wife. The correspondence between the two events is not quite as algebraic as you might think. The private affair of married persons is merely a fact of life. We are all one person, really, and what one of us experiences the other must necessarily experience, too. I should like to say that I was calm and noble when my turn in the barrel came. Unfortunately, that would be a lie. I do not like to lie.

---

[4]This is a complete lie. I had a fit and called her names and pulled her hair until she confessed. It is not clear here that this took place about a year later, when we had returned to the commune to live, while I wrote a long article on dope dealing, "Cops and Robbers" for *Rolling Stone* that Jann Wenner refused to publish. Chrissie had been unusually depressed all the previous year while we lived in Brooklyn Heights. The postman told me one day that she had her own post office box, which I refused to believe. I really did love Chrissie to the best of my very limited capacity at the time and I often think that she deserved a lot better than me or Thomas Pynchon.

I define honesty, though, as the ability to admit that you lie. I will spare you my hysterics. They lasted long enough.

The ethics are rather clear. People are not property. The hysterics over, Chrissie and I went on to attempt to reconstruct our marriage. In the course of that work, there were many conversations about what went on between the two of them that I suppose ought to be considered privileged. For the sake of the historical record, however, I do want to share a few of them with you. He was a wonderful lover, sensitive and quick, with the ability to project a mood that turned the most ordinary surroundings into a scene out of a masterful film—the reeking industrial slum of Manhattan Beach would become as seen through the eye of Antonioni, for example. Still, she found him somewhat unworldly and bookish, easily astonished by her boldness. Once, out on the freeway, she told him that we had all gone naked at the commune. He professed to find that incredible and dared her to take off her blouse right there. She did. A passing truck hooted its horn in lewd applause. He loved her Shirley Temple impersonations—"On the Good Ship Lollipop" sung and danced like a kid at a birthday party. They talked about running away together. He promised to get a job. Well, at least to move out of the cave. On their way to do the right thing, to tell me the truth, he insisted on stopping to get a pizza to calm his stomach. Then they changed their minds, fearful of one of my outrageous tantrums.

There is more and maybe I well tell it another time. I have received no letters from Tom in a long time. What did I do wrong? And those other letters—whatever did become of them? Ask the Dahill Mayflower Moving and Storage Company of Brooklyn. They are the victims of my inability to hold on to anything, sold at auction during my last long voyage through the hospitals to replace my crippled hip with one of plastic said to be almost as good as the real thing. Most probably, the auctioneer never even knew the value of those sheets of faint-blue quadrille. I miss having them, but I miss some other things more—the hipbone I was born with, an antique brass oil lamp with milk-glass shade in like-new condition purchased one sunburned summer afternoon in Elkhorn Junction, Nebraska, a gilded-wood schoolhouse pendulum clock that stopped working when my first marriage ended, a signed first edition of *The Godfather* with this inscription: "Dear Chrissie and Jules. You too can be rich and famous. See how easy it is. Mario."

BOOK CALL

If you enjoy this article and wish to show me your appreciation, you can send any book of your choice, used or new, to Apdo 1764, Cancun, Q. Roo 77501. See instructions below. I will reply personally to any letter I receive, but I will appreciate your telling me a little about yourself and what you do professionally, as it will help me understand you better.

In addition to our omnivorous reading tastes, Anita and I enjoy decent heterosexual erotica, but please don't send us anything with offensive hardcore illustrations, as it might be confiscated at customs and cause us problems. Eli, 15, is a super science nerd and has a reading level of a high school senior or better, loves science fiction. Jesse, 12, is an artist who wants to be an architect. He reads about a year or two above his age. He needs Walter Foster drawing books and any other books on technique (me too). Your old humanities and English literature text books will be thrilling for Eli and Jesse. They both read Spanish fluently, too. Faera, 25, is studying psychoanalysis [*Note:* This was written before she left for New York]. I would especially appreciate copies of *Gravity's Rainbow* and *Vineland*. Any books that are duplicates or that we don't want to keep will be donated to the library of the *Casa de la Cultura de Cancún*.

Anyone who sends us a book will receive one of my famous Awards of Merit for Service to Humanity, endorsed with his/her/its name in type, highly suitable for framing and displaying to thwart accusations of social uselessness. Be sure to include the full name in clear upper and lower case, preferably neatly typed. Send us an e-mail, too, so we can be on the look-out for your mail and let you know if it doesn't arrive within two months.

VERY IMPORTANT: Do not under any circumstances put anything illegal in anything you send us, no matter how well you think it is concealed. We don't need anything like that and we definitely do not need the very serious grief that will result if something illegal is found at customs. All packages are opened and inspected by hand, as well as by sniffer dogs, not just spot-checked. Cancun is a super high security zone and resembles Singapore in many ways more than Mexico. They are mostly looking for weapons and bombs, but if they find dope they can get quite nasty.

The quickest way to send things from the United States is by the United States Postal Service Express Mail—about $10.50 for up to 500 grams, I think. Gets here in 3-5 days. You can also use the book rate, which will get here in three to six weeks. A really great trick is to attach a registered air mail letter to the package. You then pay the registered air mail rate for the letter and the book rate for the book, but it goes air mail. If someone tells you that registered mail doesn't go to Mexico (this happened to Anita's mother), ask to speak to a supervisor.

> *The article never did make it to the full list. Pynchon-L automatically protects itself against flaming and other long-message problems by bouncing any posting over a certain length for review by the list owner. Murthy asked me what I wanted to do about this and suggested that I just leave it alone because the article was going to be available on my web site soon. If you examine the Archive, you'll find the article right here where it belongs, though, because everything posted to Pynchon-L is recorded whether it goes out to the list or not. Several people did send books, which, of course, I have not yet acknowledged, much less sent out the corresponding Awards of Merit. I'll do it as soon as I finish* Lineland.

Part 6:
Manifestations of Venus

From: Jules Siegel <jsiegel@mail.caribe.net.mx>
To: pynchon-l@waste.org
Subject: Manifestations of Venus

Preliminary Note

I have been thinking about the difficulties created by the fact that I read
Pynchon's works so many years ago—thirty, I think, for the most part. When I
receive some copies, I will try reading them again. Meanwhile, in order to
avoid confusion, I am going to respond with what I know about certain themes
and let you all decide how it applies. I hope that I am not doing something
wrong by changing the subject lines, but I want to start breaking these long
threads down into more coherent strands, so that I can keep better track of the
ideas. I am getting several dozen messages a day and many of the subject lines
no longer have very much connection to the content. Also, I am writing this
from memory and I have no easily accessible references, so I will appreciate
your tolerance (and correction) of any errors.

Bonnie L. Kyburz <Kyburz@asu.edu> wrote:

*I have always maintained that V. A Novel deals with misogyny, patriarchy, and power—
across the centuries, that Pynchon reveals something of a plot to suppress information on
the Goddess and cultures that worshipped her. There's a paper on the matter imbedded
in Tim Ware's web page. Also, one link to that paper on my page at http://
www.cas.usf.edu/english/surfus/lenore.html. It's called "She Lives in a Time of Her
Own" (yes, based upon the Erikson song).*

I agree strongly with Bonnie's points here. I think that it is important to
distinguish, however, among the various manifestations of the Goddess, of
which there are two (at least) that are relevant:

[1] The White Goddess

Extensively (and very confusingly) explored by Robert Graves in his book of the same name, this is Leucothea, associated with the Moon and, hence, the astrological sign of Cancer. In case she is unfamiliar to some of you, Leucothea is white as death, has yellow hair, an aquiline nose and is moody and changeable, like the moon. She appears in three manifestations, virgin, nymph and crone, representing new, full and waning moon as well as the pubescent, mature and post-menstrual woman. Leucothea is the goddess of lunatics and poets. She makes men mad with love, takes them off to Avalon on her white palfrey, date-rapes them repeatedly, and then drops them back into cold reality, woe-begone and naked. She is primarily a northern European manifestation, especially British/Irish/Gaelic.

She is Keats' Belle Dame Sans Merci. Leucothea is the woman you fall in love with and penetrate, being absorbed into her and dying, as the sperm loses itself in penetrating the egg. She is water, liquid, the wetness of arousal. She is not a very good fit with her astrological sign, as Cancer is the breasts and Summer, while Leucothea fits better with Spring. This may be explained by the fact that astrology began in the Fertile Crescent, where the summer would have been longer and hotter. Thus she expresses well the fleeting quality of northern summers, especially the closer you get to the Arctic Circle, the strange white light and the long, pale days, like a Swedish movie, say "Elvira Madigan"— doomed love, but hauntingly beautiful.

[2] Aphrodite

This is love as flesh, associated with Taurus and the planet Venus, the number 13, and the Greek letter Delta, which is a triangle, indicating, I think, the female pubis. I don't want to offer too many versions of her name, as I am doing this from memory, but she would be Astarte, Isis, Ashtoreth, Venus, among others. Although the statues of Aphrodite, such as the Venus de Milo, are white marble (as are most other Greek and Roman artifacts), they were once painted in flesh tones and had amethyst or other precious stones in what are now blank eyes, and were dressed in rich costumes. Too delicate to survive were the chrystosom (I'm not sure of the spelling any more) versions—cedar frames covered with ivory to simulate skin, precious stones for eyes, wigs of real hair (I think) and beautifully ornate clothing, including underthings.

Aphrodite is Mary and if you want to get a real feeling of what she must have been like, you'll find similar images in many Mexican churches, ranging in size from exquisite little dolls to life-size mannequins. She is kind and loving—though fickle (to assure the vitality of the seed by changing lovers)—and is associated with the arts of love. Aphrodite is the swelling belly, the full breasts, the mother nursing. She is earth, flesh, not the act of procreation, with all its romance, but the work of motherhood. The Bull (read also Cow, Horned Crescent) ploughs the earth.

Unlike Leucothea, who abhors homosexuality, Aphrodite is pan-sexual and orgiastic. Cross-dressing priests figure strongly in her cult. Men and women lay together naked in mass sex orgies in the ploughed fields and mingled their seed indiscriminately so that no child could know his own father. This made sure that children were not private property. They belonged to all. The Jews worshipped Saturn, not Venus. The Bible comes down so hard on homosexuality because it was treason in a time when religion and government were one, but Jewish descent is through the mother. Because my children's mothers are gentile, my children are not Jews unless they choose to convert. The greatest ode to Aphrodite ever written in the English language is Shakespeare's description of Cleopatra's arrival in Alexandria to meet Antony.

Caveat:

It is a mistake in examining the work of any artist to insist on revealing some grand architectural structure. You can do this with Escher, because he did work that way. His original cartoons (in the technical sense here) of mathematical transformations in analytical geometry are easily available. Tom is not that kind of artist in the works that I have read. Thus, I think that it is sometimes better to let him just be himself, without picking away to the under-painting of his tableaux, because his sources are often disappointingly thin. This is not always a result of lack of diligence. The sources themselves are surprisingly shallow when you examine them closely with a skeptical eye, no matter how well-embedded they are in the tapestry of conventional scholarship.

There is a tendency among scholars to mix this stuff into a confusing stew of names and places and cabalistic numerology and all that Talmudic and satanic folderol that passes for erudition. We are dealing here with many layers of myth and different dead languages and mathematical systems, alphabets and hieroglyphics, icons and pictographs. If you look at a single Tarot card, you will see a complete set of icons and glyphs and Hebrew letters. Each is a mnemonic device referring to some traditional source, itself often an encyclopedia or even a school of thought rather than a single concept or text. We have no reason to believe that any of the pre-Christian material that scholars confidently analyze has been translated correctly (or even intelligibly). The Bible has approximately 8,000 different words, of which only some 6,000 have been definitively translated. This does not necessarily mean that 25% of the Bible is conjecture, as some of these words may be inconsequential, but it does mean that any attempt to define even the literal meaning of the text (much less its poetic extensions) is doomed to endless argument. My own impression is that conventional archaeological history is a pastiche of sincere misinterpretation and very cynical religious and political "truth" correction.

You will get yourself laughed off stage at any conventional academic symposium for saying this, but it really does look as if we are dealing with material that dates back to before Noah's flood, which I am sure was a historical fact best explained by the theories of Immanuel Velikovsky. At one time a vast and highly evolved civilization on Earth was almost entirely destroyed by cosmic cataclysms that occurred within the historical memory of man. Much meaning disappeared along with its physical context. Graves very convincingly argued in *The Greek Myths*, his definitive translation and superb exegesis, that the Greek myths are verbal descriptions of long-lost ancient murals. He thought the original meanings were historical and political and that the changes and misinterpretations were designed to rationalize (and disguise) the transition from matriarchal to patriarchal systems.

THIS MAY VERY WELL BE TRUE, but what if the murals recorded astronomical events rather than human history? Let's look at the charming myth of Aphrodite's affair with Mars, the entwined lovers discovered in Vulcan's golden net as the rest of the gods look on. Excuse me if I am mixing Greek and Roman names here. Examine the physical descriptions of the gods, principally Mars, who is ruddy, as is the planet, and Aphrodite, who is hot, as is her planet. Vulcan is lame and a smith. As you may know, there is some reason to believe that a planet called Vulcan once existed in what is now the asteroid belt. Velikovsky claimed (to the best of my memory) that a comet appeared out of the Red Spot in Jupiter, nearly colliding with Mars and coming so close to the Earth that a cosmic spark passed between the object and Earth. It settled into an orbit around the sun and became the planet Venus. If there are any Velikovsky experts here, I hope they will correct this scheme, but let us accept it in broad outline for the sake of the argument.

The correct meaning of the myth, then, is a verbal description of a mural (or other lost pictorial record) showing the planets Venus and Mars caught in merged gravitational fields (the net) with a damaged iron planet and the rest of the planets in the background. First it was written down (or spoken, perhaps) in its literal meaning, which everyone at the time understood. By the time we read it, it has been translated several times and what were once planets have been changed into persona.

Cross-cultural translation is a treacherous business even when you can call up a Chinese friend and check out the meaning. But across eons?

I don't want everyone to get mad at me, but I think you have to begin to accept the fact that Tom's grasp of things that he glibly sets down as if he were a master of the material is usually quite superficial, based on reading anything from, say, Bible Comics to learned journals. This is not a criticism, but a description. The effect he achieves is often exquisite, but you are not necessarily going to get very far by examining how he achieves it, and, in fact, will be lucky to retain the original thrill you felt when you let his incantations charm you across the borders of reality into his mostly imaginary landscapes.

A lot of times, I think, he is talking in tongues. Usually, that is when he is at his greatest, whereas such highly researched sections as Malta and Africa can be deadly. When he does get that romantic enchantment going he is often departing from historical reality. The Herero women were not beautiful by our standards. They had huge buttocks—grotesque, really, to the modern Anglo-European eye—and were probably the inspiration for the fabled Callipygians, which meant the people with beautiful buttocks. This is a problem that many modern black women have just had to live with. Their inherited physical beauty is of another time and another culture.

Ashanti women (and men) had bodies like Roman statues—think of Muhammad Eli, only black as coal. The Masai were tall and thin, our basketball stars. I think it is difficult for us to realize how physically different the various African peoples were from each other. Perhaps Craig Clark can help us on this. Meanwhile, I feel that in *V.*, as in erotic literature, facts that might interfere with romance tend to get left in the bathroom with the tube of spermicidal jelly and the diaphragm case. And *V.* is in very many ways an erotic novel, not only or merely an erotic novel, but mostly an erotic novel—a literary equivalent of Milo Manera's dreamy illustrated novels, lots of nakedness, no more than mere hints of penetration.

V. is an inspired work—in the sense of Goddess-inspired—and inspiration does not lend itself to rational examination. I would say that the Pynchon scholar will do best by attempting to identify what a given item might have meant to Tom, where he got it, and what it means in Tom's schema, to the extent that this can be identified, as I don't think he always has a schema.

Despite this, Bonnie has the right idea, I think, but she should not fall into the trap of taking this theme too literally or too seriously. Pynchon is not necessarily writing about the Goddess in an organized and literal way. He is her instrument and she is talking through him and there could be quite a bit of static on the line. This interpretation will help you understand the enchantment you feel again and again when reading *V.* It is incantation, a word etymologically almost equivalent to enchantment, getting you under its spell.

I once asked Chester Anderson, a great magician, founder of The Communication Company, to explain to me how I could use Magick to make money. "Magick isn't about money, Jules," he replied. "It's about ecstasy." In case that doesn't make sense in the present context, think about money as accounting. *V.* is about (and the product of) ecstasy. I don't think the principles of accounting (in the sense of rational academic scholarship) will always be very useful here.

---

tstanton@nationalgeographic.com wrote:

Whoa, dude! I was with you on the goddess stuff & biblical translation business, but Velikovsky??? You're right, the symposium just became the Komedy Kassle!

Yikes! Velikovsky is right up there with the other pseudo-scientists. No evidence, no support, but a whopping good story. Comets don't emerge from the red spot, carom off planets like pool balls, and then turn into another planet.

Sorry, not gonna bite on this one…

JULES REPLIED: Of course not. Actually, you just did. Have you ever read Velikovsky and looked at his critics? I have. Carefully. Skeptically. What an unbelievable case of academic lynching! Really disgusting.

When do scientists quit claiming that their views are Truth and everything else is pseudo-science? Velikovsky has a strong hypothesis. Maybe your guys have strong hypotheses too. But that's all they are: informed (sort of) speculation.

One question: Where did the vegetation found in the stomachs of still-preserved Siberian mastodons uncovered in 10,000+ years-old snow come from?

Always wondered about that. Appreciate an answer. Really.

---

davemarc <davemarc@panix.com> wrote:

JULES WRITES: *The Herero women were not beautiful by our standards. [...] I think it is difficult for us to realize how physically different the various African peoples were from each other.*

On an international list such as this one, it's often unclear what is meant when a participant uses words like "our" and "us." I, for one, do not wish to be passively associated as agreeing with the remarks Jules makes in the material quoted above.

JULES: Why? I meant people of our time and culture. I didn't say it was impossible. I said it was difficult. How many people on the list are aware of the differing physical characteristics of African regional groups—or world regional groups? Is the male (and female, to a great extent) Anglo-European hung up in the Venus de Milo-to-*Playboy* body style image or not?

The very fact that Pynchon does not include physical descriptions of his protagonists in the African sequences, although he does elsewhere frequently in *V*, is revealing. Did he not know? Or did he airbrush it? Is he an occult racist?

I know that given the same material I could have made it clear what these physical differences meant to the lovers and I would have done it in a way that revealed the beauty that they saw in each other, especially because it was different from our (see above) own culturally installed prejudices. He hid from it.

At the same time, the point is well-taken. Cross-cultural references have to be absolutized or generalized where necessary, just like links. I'll keep that in mind and I appreciate the insight.

Joe Varo <vjvaro@erie.net> wrote:

I most definitely do not want to fan the above two embers into a flame war, but I think that a comment is called for here.

First of all, I think that Mr. Siegel does rather explicitly say who are the "our" and "us" to which he refers, i.e. "the modern Anglo-European eye."

It seems pretty clear to me whom he's referring to and it also seems pretty clear to me that he is expressing his own opinion. I don't see why anyone would fear being "passively associated" with his opinion.

If the need to publicly disavow oneself from Mr. Siegel's comment is so strong, then perhaps one ought to publicly disavow oneself from Pynchon for his comments regarding "Negroes" in *Gravity's Rainbow*, such as the toilet scene wherein it is suggested that they're sodomites.

I don't know if this is a case of someone being miffed about Mr. Siegel posting his comments about the list's "raison d'etre" or a case of political correctness gone berserk.

From:	Diana York Blaine <dyb0001@jove.acs.unt.edu>
To:	davemarc@panix.com
Subject:	What's wrong with being pc?

God bless you for your comments about the creepy Jules and his big-butted big-breasted Playboynoid fantasies. Barf. That this egomaniac has been living rent free in my brain for several minutes each day has made me scrub extra hard in the shower. But the overwhelmingly sympathetic tone of the other readers (except my good buddy Mascaro) has made me despair of pointing out how obsessive and sexist his postings have become (believe it or not women aren't particularly thrilled by someone who cannot tell the difference between humans who happen to be genetically female and white goddesses—particularly from someone who rails about NOW apropos of nothing except his own apparent misogyny.) So again, thanks for pointing out that JS does not speak with the universal voice esp. since he's so prone to pontification. You'll notice

BTW what Chrissie thinks about his sensitivity towards women, and that little psychodrama came to us through the unreliable narrator himself (shades of HH?).

I don't know where the comment about NOW came from. I've looked through all my messages and I can't find a single mention, much less any railing. "HH" is Humbert Humbert, for those who asked.

Joe Varo <vjvaro@erie.net>

God bless you for your comments about the creepy Jules and his big-butted big-breasted Playboynoid fantasies.

Personal epithets? This really advances your cause.

Barf.

Oh, like, groady, gag me with a spoon.

That this egomaniac has been living rent free in my brain for several minutes each day has made me scrub extra hard in the shower.

Real easy solution here: either present a sustained, logical argument against his posts or just delete all messages from Jules Siegel before reading them. I suppose that as long as you're subscribed to Pynchon-L you can't keep his messages from occupying space in your e-mail box, but if he gets into your brain, well, that's your own fault.

Though I don't completely agree with davemarc's post at least I can respect it; he gave reasons rather than words like "creepy" and "barf."

So again, thanks for pointing out that JS does not speak with the universal voice esp. since he's so prone to pontification.

Again, where does anyone get the notion that Siegel is speaking for everyone on this list, everyone in the world, every whoever?

Okay, yes, he used the words "our," "us" and "Anglo-European." Perhaps he should have prefaced everything with an explicit "IMHO," but that's how I understood it to begin with, as his opinion.

But to refer to someone as "creepy" or a "misogynist" is simply name-calling.

I really think this is all a bit of an over-reaction...but then, perhaps I'm over-reacting myself.

> IMHO *is a* TLA—*a Three Letter Acronym, in this case meaning In My Humble Opinion. I like three letter acronyms about as much as I like emoticons. Here's a list of basic Three Letter Acronym's followed by emoticons, also called "Smileys," which I compiled from postings to the discussion list of Public Relations and Corporate Communications Academics and Professionals <prforum@listserv.iupui.edu> by Brady Chatfield <bchatfie@pcshs.com>, Hector Hereter <hereter1@airmail.net>, Marc Snyder <masnyder@eureka.qc.ca> and Dick Weltz <DickWeltz@aol.com>*

AFAIK	*As Far As I Know*
AKA	*Also Known As*
ASAP	*As Soon As Possible*
BRB	*Be right back*
BTW	*By the way*
CYA	*See you*
FAQ	*Frequently asked questions*
FYI	*For Your Information*
FWIW	*For What It's Worth*
FUBAR	*Fucked Up Beyond All Recognition*
GD&R	*Grinning, Ducking and Running (After snide remark)*
HTH	*Hope this helps*
IANAL	*I am not a lawyer (but...)*
IDK	*I don't know*
IMHO	*In my humble opinion*
IYKWIM	*If You Know What I Mean*
IYKWIMAITYD	*If You Know What I Mean And I Think You Do*
LOL	*Laughing out loud*
NE1	*Anyone*

GD&R—*Grinning, Ducking and Running*

OTF	*On the floor*
OTFL	*On the floor laughing*
OTOH	*On The Other Hand*
PITA	*Pain In The Ass*
PMFJI	*Pardon Me for Jumping in*
PMJI	*Pardon My Jumping In*
ROTFL	*Rolling On the Floor Laughing*
RTFM	*Read The Fucking Manual*
TIA	*Thanks In Advance*
TPTB	*The Powers That Be*
TTFN	*Ta Ta For Now*
SOHF	*Sense Of Humor Failure*
WRT	*With Respect To*
WYSIWYG	*What You See Is What You Get*
YMMV	*Your Mileage May Vary*
	(You may not have the same luck I did)
YWIA	*You're welcome in advance*

Basic Smilies

:-)	*Standard Smilie*
;-)	*Winking smilie.*
;-(	*Sad smilie*
:-D	*Laughing*
:-@	*Screaming*
:-|	*Hmmm...don't know what to think*
:-X	*My lips are sealed*
:-*	*Kissing*
:-+	*Ooooohhhh!!!*

---

mascaro@humnet.ucla.edu

This academic/non-academic duality polarity dichotomy is nonsense. Can't—academics—who don't seem to be spoken of very highly—read for fun too? I agree completely that a lot of academic criticism is bullshit, but so is a lot of non-academic opinionizing (cf. As The Tom Turns, our very own p-list soap opera!) We all have to separate the pigs from the pokes, you know.

But really, does wondering how something works mean you are missing the experience? Does believing that knowing how something works enhances your fun in digging it make one an effete egghead? Does knowing what a cello sounds like mean you can't appreciate a symphony? silly silly

---

Greg Montalbano <opsgmm@uccvma.ucop.edu>

I second this. I may be the least "academic" of all the readers on this list; came upon Pynchon's works as they were published, and read (and re-read) them all for no other reason than the fun, the challenge, the wonder, and the joy of it. Couldn't really imagine being "forced" to read them for a class.

JULES: I was speaking generically. What I mean by academic art is art that is created for the academy, which is not the same as work studied by the academy. I do think, however, that his works that I read had a decidedly academic flavor, in the sense of deliberate obscurity, heavy symbolic structure, and reliance on library research. There was quite a vogue in the Fifties for studying the scientific meaning and historical background of John Donne's "conceits." Tom's short story, "Entropy," seems to me to reflect that trend. I know that his fluid use of scientific metaphor was warmly greeted by reviewers and scholars. Close textual analysis was also a big thing. *V.* reads to me almost as if written for elucidation. I am not criticizing him for this. I also did some of it when I was younger, principally in my poetry. I was apologizing for my lack of interest in much of his work by describing my own personal and professional preferences. I would be flattered by academic analysis of my own work, but I don't expect it, as I made a different set of choices.

Murthy Yenamandra <yenamand@cs.umn.edu> wrote:

JULES SIEGEL WRITES, *among other things: "[...] From what I see here, many of the people on the list have not been able to get through* Gravity's Rainbow *and, in fact, are here in order to understand it better."*

Just wanted to point out that getting through *Gravity's Rainbow* and appreciating it are not really incompatible with wanting to understand it better (may be even a prerequisite). In fact, I'd wager that most people (academic or not) on this list fell in love with it on the first read and kept coming up with new stuff on every re-read. But it's also true that everyone has their own idea of what is clear and/or accessible, so debating it here is probably futile (not that I want to discourage anyone from doing so).

JULES: This is going to be another lengthy reply. I'm sorry if I seem long-winded and self-reflective in these explanations, but I am trying to be precise. I am responding to the very evident seriousness of your comments by telling you how my time looked to me and how I participated in its construction, as I see that much of your difficulty with Tom's writing is a result of living in a vastly expanded time zone. *Gravity's Rainbow* is in one place. You're in another. You need a time machine to get to where he was when he wrote it.

Let's go back to Cornell. I don't think that Tom necessarily created his work for the academy. I do know that he studied writing at Cornell. I only spent one very unhappy year there and wrote one short story which I submitted to *Epoch*, the literary journal. It was rejected without comment. I went over and talked to the faculty member who edited the publication and he told me in a very frosty and condescending manner that it was "too slick." When I challenged him to explain what he meant, all he could offer was a single phrase, in which I described a gift to a girl as having "the unmistakable sheen of sterling silver."

The story, which I lost a long time ago, was a very naturalistic description of a young man's unrequited love set at a tawdry middle-class students party in The Bronx. There was no symbolism, no learned references, no complex language: just the bare relation of what was said, what things looked like and how the boy felt. Today, I believe they call this minimalism, although I don't know if that would include how he felt.

Tom was always a diligent student. He got straight As. I think it is quite clear that his early work, as I pointed out in a previous posting, reflects his academic training. What many found interesting was the way he combined very contemporary material, including scientific thinking, with the kind of writing methods then taught in college literature courses. Academic scholarship is useful for uncovering the meaning of works that have been clouded by time, or are otherwise difficult to appreciate. Because of the evolution of the English language, you can't really understand Shakespeare without a gloss. Some of his terms have opposite meanings today. Then there is the problem of establishing the original text. I'm sure you all have been through these courses and understand what I'm saying.

Everyone wants to get good marks in school. More than that, most writers begin without a plan or a life theme. If you go to the University of Missouri they teach you how to write newspaper copy. If you went to Cornell in 1954, they taught you how to write the kind of works that they studied, not necessarily in a direct pedagogic formula, but by implication. Literature was important because it was studied, it seemed; therefore, to obtain approval, one wrote works that lent themselves to study. This is where Pynchon began. I don't know where he has gone. I was taught how to write by working writers and editors: Mario Puzo, Bruce Jay Friedman, among others. These are two very different disciplines. They are not mutually incompatible, but there is a great deal of antagonism on both sides. Academics once held popular writing (and art) in contempt. This aroused resentment among writers and artists who did not fit their criteria.

Example:

That's Not Art, That's Illustration

Almost everybody is an artist these days. Rock-and-roll singers are artists. So are movie directors, performance artists, makeup artists, tattoo artists, con artists, and rap artists. Madonna is an artist because she explores her own sexuality. Snoop Doggy Dogg is an artist because he explores other people's sexuality. Victims who express their pain are artists. So are guys in prison who express themselves on shirt cardboard. Even consumers are artists when they express themselves in their selection of commodities. The only people left in America who seem not to be artists are illustrators.

—Brad Holland, from his book *Illustration America,*
as excerpted in *The Atlantic,* July, 1996.

To see this debate more clearly, allow me to move the discussion to another field, Top 40 radio. Bob Dylan was a campus hero when he wrote mass market songs using the methods of the folk song and acoustic instruments. When he turned to rock and electric guitar, he was literally howled off the stage at Newport. At about the same time, 1965, I wrote "The Big Beat," for *Cavalier,* a *Playboy* knock-off, in which I used academic methods of cultural analysis on Top 40 music. Other journalists—especially the British—were edging in the same direction, but my piece was acknowledged at the time as having defined and synthesized a new way of looking at popular music.

During the years that followed, rock criticism evolved into an industry. People began writing music to fit this industry, which before long became a subset of the academy. Believe me when I tell you that a course in the cultural significance of rock would have been a joke in 1963. I am not saying that this began with my article, but that my article was an expression of an emerging consciousness, exemplified by "A Whiter Shade of Pale," the consummate synthesis of classical style and modern content. The Academy hit the Top 40 Number One with a Bullet.

Pynchon, I think, is kind of a literary version of Procul Harum. He is a university-trained writer whose training is reflected in his methods and whose interests are reflected in his content. He requires elucidation because his interests are so varied, ranging from lowdown jokes to highbrow science. This elucidation has become even more important as his sources have become clouded by time. Many of you have no idea what the Sixties were like. You're too young. Few Americans my age need banana peel smoking explained. How many of any of us have had the freedom or inclination to spend day after day in the library pursuing anything at all that interested us at the moment? Tom did, so what was easy and familiar to him was often obscure to anyone else. He has become a puzzle in his own lifetime not so much because he deliberately wrote puzzles, but also because the frenetic evolution of modern information technology and marketing has speeded up the passage of perceived time.

Jeff Meikle <meikle@mail.utexas.edu> wrote:

Jules says: "Many of you have no idea what the Sixties were like. You're too young. Few Americans my age need banana peel smoking explained."

Hmmm… anybody here remember Clifford Irving's exclusive biography of reclusive tycoon Howard Hughes? Turned out to be a hoax. Then there were the so-called Hitler diaries. A hoax as well, though authenticated by authorities. Now that Jules has revealed his werewolf (vampire?) fangs, I don't mind opining that he hasn't told us anything that couldn't be cleverly extrapolated from the public record. If They can get you asking the wrong questions, They don't have to worry about the answers.

JULES: I'm not a hoax. Get your dukes up, dude, when you say that. Where are these public records and what do they say?

You'll find that much of what is in the public record comes from me in the first place.

Playboy Editorial Director Arthur Kretchmer and his wife, Patricia, met Judith Pynchon, Tom's sister, when we dated in New York in 1964 or 65. She was studying in Pittsburgh and drove up to see me in her MG, which was broken into while we were at a movie opening. All her clothes were stolen, and she was wearing a formal dress, so we went over to their place to borrow a dress from Pat. Didn't fit.

Lots of people at Cornell knew we were friends. You want to tell me Chrissie's a fake, too? Show me a fact that could have been extrapolated from the public record, I describe two different apartments in Manhattan Beach, neither of which were ever revealed before my piece appeared.

Better, call Tom's father (I hope he's still around—really wonderful man) and ask him if I exist. Ask his former agent, Candida Donadio, if she knows Jules Siegel and listen to her whine about how when I heard she was in the hospital with diabetes circulatory problems requiring her toes to be amputated, I wrote her: "Cutting off your toes to spite your feet, Candida?"

—The Werewolf

At this point, the discussion on the themes of political correctness and academics degenerated into a mass free-for-all flame-fest, too extensive and tedious to reprint. If you ever need an example of a

full-fledged literary and political flame war it will be well worth
your while to examine the Pynchon-L Archive for late October and
early November, 1996.

Michael Glosup <mglosup@randomc.com> wrote:

Before you all send tons of books to an American expatriate in a Mexican
resort community might I suggest organizations more deserving of your lar-
gesse.

    1. Your local public library obviously. They can be picky about what they
accept though.

    2. Your local penal institution. Prison libraries are seriously underfunded, in
some jurisdictions they are not funded at all and rely exclusively on donations.
Prison libraries become increasingly more important as other *amenities* for
inmates are cut. Copies of Anarchist Cookbook and US Army Special Forces
training manuals would be greatly appreciated.

    3. If you feel compelled to ship your books overseas please send them to
International Book Bank, 815 Central Ave, Linthicum, MD 21090. This non-
profit organization supplies books to Third World public educational institutions, benefiting poor people without Uma Thurmanesque wives in Caribbean party towns. Thanks.

JULES: What a wonderful person. How about it folks? Should we just remove
the piece? How about if I put some kind of a meter on it and charge by the
view or download? You can always count on someone to ruin your day here,
can't you?

    Why should this sweetheart read my stuff free?

    This is the single most disgusting thing that I have come across in my short
time on the Internet. What a worm.

From: mascaro@humnet.ucla.edu
Subject: Silver bullets for the big bad—

Jules Siegel— Despite your command that I reply interlinearly, I don't want to.
Is that O.K.? You certainly trashed me pretty good in that—werewolf—opus

"Where do you come off with this hubristic air of having special access because you can connect us with somebody who was intimate with him a long time ago?"

of yours, even got me laughing a little. But I have been down that road before. I don't think I resorted to the kind of nasty little name calling you seem to excel in, but I understand how thin skinned a guy can get to be when almost his only claim to fame is that TRP stopped talking to him in 1968. (uh-oh, I'm getting in a fight again, and I really don't want to do that). Your reply to George Haberberger re: the grandmother reference really speaks for itself in showing how you have some trouble distinguishing between a writer and his work, or between fact and fiction (duh, yes Diana I might be offending the professoriate by speaking on such a simplistic level):

JULES WROTE: *Never been much of a Hunter S. Thomspon fan, as I always felt he gave drugs a bad name, as well as encouraging by example stupid overdosing, mixing the wrong things, and generally abusing substances that are really antidotes to the general horror of our time. He wasn't a psychedelic prophet, he was a tawdry glutton.*

So if you can defame Thompson (and so ludicrously misunderstand gonzoism in all of its beauty) for no reason at all, I guess I can poke at you a little. But I really was conceding to the wishes of this list when I tried to back off criticizing you. I feel the scorn of social disapprobation as much as anybody. But the notion that I think of P. as some sort of god and resent the fact that you (of all people) are here to show us his—human—side, is ridiculous. Of course he's just a guy. He's also one of the 20th century's best writers. Those two facts are completely separate, in my opinion. We are curious about his life, sure, but where do you come off with this hubristic air of having special access because you can connect us with somebody who was intimate with him a long time ago? I am bugged by your egoism in this regard. For proof I refer to the number of queries re P. that you answer with some version of: "I can best answer that by talking about myself." But, hey, Mr. Werewolf, as I said, the list likes what you are doing, and doesn't think my concerns are very strong. I yield to that pressure.

Hey, that—pampers—thing, wow, am I cut or what?

Regarding the Drug question: I think you have repeatedly connected P.'s writing to his drug use, and you admit to doing so, and I think that is an uncool thing to do, Not because I don't like drugs, far from it, but because it gives idiots ammunition to criticize P. (I have heard professors do this). More importantly, it reifies drug use inappropriately. Let's talk about P.'s avoidance of Pork as a source of his artistic vision to see how preposterous all such speculation is. What's in GR is there because he wanted it there, not because he was too stoned to tell. You imply otherwise, I think. But if I am wrong, please show me and I will apologize.

O.K. big chill now, Siegel la werewolf. I am probably almost as old as you are, and I went through the same times. If you wanna keep fighting, I'll be there, but maybe we can cool it now.

—john m

Jules Siegel <jsiegel@caribe.net.mx> wrote:

I understand how thin skinned a guy can get to be when almost his only claim to fame is that TRP stopped talking to him in 1968.

I think they have adult-sized Pampers, don't they? Check out my resume, doo-doo brain. It's not my fault you only know some big names. Now, of course, if I were a capitalist sell-out I'd be big time famous, too, wouldn't I? I *chose* obscurity. What did you do to be so small?

Please wipe carefully before posting again.

I have no luck today. He *can't* check my resume. There's some problem with the links. It began when I revised it to include a pointer to the infamous Thomas Pynchon profile that just caused me to receive so much heartwarming mail today. Do you think that Tom *is* online and not only that he's become a master hacker and put pixel goo in my resume? More likely that I'm just inept.

Heartwarming, really. Gave folks a way to show their appreciation. Big mistake, it seems. Undeserving. Bad resume, too.

*I still like to say, 'To the showers with the Jew!'
when I leave the room to bathe.*

Jeff Rice <afn49457@afn.org> wrote:

Was this interview supposed to be about Pynchon or Jules Siegel? I got the impression that it was about the latter.

JULES: Please don't be thick. It was about our reactions to Pynchon. You want to understand these reactions, you better try to understand us, right?

These kind of responses always remind me of pornography fans—just the hot spots please.

The interview was a literary document in its own right. You get the set and setting, not just the hot stuff.

If you want a point-by-point analysis of how dumb your question is please send an e-mail message with "A question for the Werewolf" in the subject line. Grrr.

---

plachazu@ccnet.com wrote:

Aw come on! Jules really has put up with a lot from us. For one thing I particularly liked his very sensible observations on depth of detail (real or only apparent) in TRP's fiction, and the vanity (quite possibly) of pursuing these often rather accidental writerly tropes and meanderings down to their most basic roots. What's the motivation for doing so (I ask), and at what point of excess does it become simply a geek's game without any further literary or aesthetic relevance?

I also enjoyed his survey of forms of the "white goddess." And as for Chrissie winning the dance contest in Manhattan Beach, a "White Goddess in hot flesh and teenage underwear," I only wish that I had been there. How about the statement that "Bianca, obviously, is based on Chrissie?" There was speculation on this list during the last year or so about Bianca's age. Some p-listers even made her out to be sixteen or so. Because of this, and also because I never knew Chrissie, I'd like to hear more from Jules about why the identification of Bianca with Chrissie is (to him) so obvious.

—jm

Jeff Rice <afn49457@afn.org>

Don't take it too personally, Jules, Jim, or any other member of this list, but my point is that this list has turned into the Mickey Mouse Fan Club. What shirt does TRP wear? Does he wipe? Which side of the bed does he sleep on? Then, most of the answers thrown back (especially this interview) or less about the subject that everyone is dying to gossip about but more about the person who is doing the interview and who admits: he doesn't read TRP's work; and hasn't seen him or spoken to him in quite some time. Go back and read the interview. See where it is no longer about TRP but the relationship between the interviewer and Chrissie.

The list can take any discussion its members want to. But I'm not sure that I understand this quest for *People* magazine, I read it in the *Star*, need to know every little aspect of a reclusive writer's life. I think you're right: it has become a geek's game without literary reference.

Steven Maas (CUTR) wrote:

Jules quotes Chrissie as saying Pynchon was (is?) anti-Semitic. I wondered if you (Jules) think this is true or do you think Chrissie was mistaken or was just saying this out of anger.

JULES REPLIES: Could be true. Also, he could have been just making silly jokes. My brother and I used to do that all the time. I still love to say, "To the showers with the Jew!" when I leave the room to bathe. I'm the only Yid in this family. When they get on me for something and I can't defend myself I accuse them of being kike haters. We Jews are allowed to do this. I would have to know what he said in order to answer your question, but I don't think he was ever known for good taste in humor. I tend to suspect that Chrissie was picking up on something real.

'So, black women miss out not just once because they do not conform to the white standard of beauty but twice because they do not even approximate to the standard against which black women qua black women are judged.'

To:	davemarc <davemarc@panix.com>
From:	Jules Siegel <jsiegel@mail.caribe.net.mx>
Subject:	Re: pynchon's misogyny
cc:	Andrew Dinn <andrew@cee.hw.ac.uk>

DAVEMARC <DAVEMARC@PANIX.COM> WROTE: *Something that puzzled me about Jules's callipygian post was my knowledge (based on his other postings) of his affection for Crumb, since Crumb (the artist, the art, the following) struck me as a clear and familiar example of one area in which Jules's generalizing about modern-day perceptions of beauty was not valid.*

Actually, you make my point here. Even Crumb himself realizes that his preference is not mainstream. As I pointed out in something way back when, he wrote me a long letter in his own handwriting talking about it as a psychological problem.

Crumb doesn't flinch from Angelfood McSpade's blackness, does he? I think he even romanticizes it a little. The humor comes from the fact that he looks at *all* physical stereotypes and satirizes them with an affection for the line that cancels out a lot of the negative qualities. Angelfood is a metaphor for all of us here outside the Anglo-European ideal. I am a black-listed Jewish cripple living in a third-world resort. Believe me when I tell you that I have reason to feel marginal.

"Only four more years of licking out these toilets and I will be a white person," she says at the end of a take on the noble savage being "civilized" by Skid Row lechers.

Sometimes I feel the same way and even say it out loud to my not-very-Uma-Thurmanesque wife (Uma should be so beautiful): "Only forty more years of licking out toilets and I will be a white person." Like Michael Glosup, for example?

The issue in the Herero sequence is specifically the airbrushing of physical characteristics. I think that the sequence is there because he came across this research and was struck by how it predicted the Nazi era. He puts a kind of sugar coating of Socialist Realism on it because it is propaganda and he doesn't want anything to get in the way that might prejudice the reader's identification with the victims.

I was also glad to see your points about our exchange. It was a model of civilized behavior. I myself failed to understand how I figured in any of the bitterness that followed.

No post, ok? No have to say this more, yes?

Andrew Dinn wrote:

I don't think the presence of this stereotype argues against Jules point, in fact the reverse. No black woman looks anything like Angelfood McSpade. Some white women do approximate vaguely to *Playboy* girls (even the models don't actually approximate physically to what appears in the mag thanks to all the prior preening, pruning and airbrushing—we will ignore the stuff that goes by name of biographical blurb). So, black women miss out not just once because they do not conform to the white standard of beauty but twice because they do not even approximate to the standard against which black women *qua* black women are judged.

JULES REPLIES: Hear! Hear!

Do they really do that in Parliament?

You're wrong about the *Playboy* models, by the way. They're even more beautiful in person. I don't think they do much airbrushing, if any. It's mostly make-up, lighting and really brilliant camera work.

Also, I don't know if any black women look like Angelfood McSpade, but some do look like the photographs of Herero women I've seen. I made love to one when I was much younger. I felt quite overwhelmed, as I am physically slight.

We see them here in Cancun (an absolutely non-racist resort), too. This is really a strange problem to try to explain, but physical body types are subject to discrimination.

I'm sure I could dig up the demographics on this, but I would bet anything that people who do not fit the Anglo-European industrial propaganda standard have less of a chance of emerging from the ghetto. So you don't see those with defiantly negroid features and body types as much, but rather those with the required facial and physical structure.

From:	Murthy Yenamandra <yenamand@cs.umn.edu>
Subject:	GRGR(3): Some more questions…
To:	pynchon-l@waste.org (pynchon-l)

Here are a few more questions/ideas about GRGR(3) to divert all you folks who don't want to talk about Pynchon's personal life.

1) (V36.10) "[…] though herself too young to know *that*, to know, like Pirate, what the lyrics to "Dancing in the Dark" are *really* about…"

Well, what are they about?

2) (V36.35) "you've come and taken me off on your pirate ship. A girl of good family and the usual repressions. You've raped me. And I'm the Red Bitch of the High Seas…"

Why the "Red Bitch of the High Seas"? A throw-away rape fantasy to boot….

More questions snipped.

Jules Siegel <jsiegel@mail.caribe.net.mx> **wrote:**

Hah-HAH! You can't escape Pynchon Confidential. Here's a great personal nugget: I think Chrissie told me once that she and Pynchon made this skit up together. She said they used to dress up in costumes like kids and act out little erotic playlets like this.

brett coley <bcoley@vnet.ibm.com> **wrote:**

This is a 40's song, Artie Shaw I think. I don't know about the meaning, seems like it could be sex, or death.

Are you unable to understand why they're laughing? You need a humor implant!

Jules Siegel <jsiegel@mail.caribe.net.mx> wrote:

Correcto! Great song. "When the tune ends we're dancing in the dark." I think this one means exactly what it says on the face of it—romantic couple dancing in the dark.

Andrew Dinn <andrew@cee.hw.ac.uk> wrote:

Oh no. Not on the Pynchon list it doesn't.

From:	Jules Siegel <jsiegel@pdc.caribe.net.mx>
To:	pynchon-l@waste.org
Subject:	Playboy Article Pointer

Try: `http://www.caribe.net.mx/siegel/pynchon.htm`

My resume links may not be working yet, but this should get you to the article. I can't check this now. Eli is going to send this out to you, as I can't even look at the Internet today without precipitating a lentil soup crisis.

Given yesterday's response to my book hustle, I will need some ideas on how to program the meter. Nine hundred number? Hook up with Amateur Hardcore Downloads and have them market and bill for me?

I am still so ticked off about this that I couldn't sleep last night. The Award of Merit that I offered as a Thank You gift would have no value, of course, because my only claim to fame is that Thomas Pynchon stopped talking to me in 1968.

That's right, that book-hustling party animal Jules Siegel is working the Pynchon literary tea party for a *bundle* in a hoax that makes the Piltdown Man scam look trivial. Does anyone else remember him on those *National Geographic* out-of-the-swamp artist's renderings of the evolutionary chain leading to the emergence of *Homo scientist* (comes right after *Homo sapiens*, having traded wisdom for knowledge)? SEC pops big pseudo-science junk book scheme on Internet.

I am sending this to the list so that anyone else who did not get a copy of the article can send me pleading, respectful messages assuring me of their loyalty in all arguments from now until the end of time, forsaking all others till unsubscribe do us part. Is that clear?

Not only am I going to continue hustling for books, but also I am going to start selling Humor Implants. This remarkable product is currently in the pre-beta phase at Siegel & Children Third World Slave Labor Industries SA de CV. Clip it behind your ear and you will instantly be able to understand jokes, wisecracks, witty remarks, satire and irony.

Do you hear what they are saying, but are you unable to understand why they're laughing? You need a humor implant! We have a gigantic marketing plan ready to explode on Pynchon-L. Just working on the final details. The big problem is to get the thing down to the size of a grain of salt.

Diana York Blaine <dybo001@jove.acs.unt.edu> wrote:

...creepy Jules and his big-butted big-breasted Playboynoid fantasies...

Actually, I prefer women with small breasts, but like many perverts (male and female) I do admire well-rounded bottoms. As I'm sure you've guessed, I detest brainy women though. Anita and Chrissie won't even understand how you've insulted them, the stupid little things.

That this egomaniac has been living rent free in my brain for several minutes each day has made me scrub extra hard in the shower.

Love is like that, isn't it? Makes you want to be clean. I think about you, too. Just my type.

...he's so prone to pontification.

Readers expect some pontification from writers. I don't smoke a pipe and I never worked as a steamfitter or a longshoreman, so I have to pontificate a little more to fill out my image.

[INTERNET VIEWERS: if this posting makes you angry, don't forget to apply for your Humor Implant Sales Kit. We expect to be sending out the first beta copies when the big book hustle campaign winds down.

—REPLY: HTTP://WWW.RIPOFF.NET/SPAMS/#51754]

From: Gardener Cady <cadyg@elwha.evergreen.edu>
To: Jules Siegel <jsiegel@pdc.caribe.net.mx>
Subject: Oh, Yes Please!

Would you please E-mail your Playboy article to me? It would make me ever so happy. I hope you don't get too bogged down with requests.

—Gardy Cady
Olympia, WA.

From: "Henry M" <gravity@dcez.nicom.com>
Subject: Siegel List

MASCARO VS. SIEGEL — Rated R for Redundant

SIEGEL VS. PYNCHON — Fought in two rings separated by decades and continents—no contest

TOO MUCH SIEGEL — Too much "too much Siegel."

Concerning the current cultural insensitivity question:

Have "we" become so reactive that we can't say something that is unfortunately the viewpoint of a majority of not only most white American males, but, I believe most other Euro types, black and white, male and female, without using a parenthetical statement that it is unfortunate?

<namdeirf@gwis2.circ.gwu.edu> wrote:

Either this Jules Siegel guy is the biggest huckster since P. T. Barnum or the greatest savior since…well, I'm not religious, so I'll let you pick the appropriate idol….

Nonetheless, what entertainment it is to hear all of you bitching back and forth to one another about a man who may or may not know someone whose name may or may not be Thomas Pynchon who may or may not be one of the twentieth century's greatest writers.

Gee, how tenuous the Internet is…

I hope my subtle sardonicism is missed on no one.

—David Nevin Friedman

BTW, before I get flamed myself (I can feel the heat coming) I do not mean to disparage Michael Glosup's suggestion of what to do with excess books. I mean merely to disparage those petty arguments that cannot be substantiated, whether the argument be initiated by or directed to Mr. Siegel. If you are so compelled to disagree with the man, rock n roll, as they say, and if you want to listen to what he has to say, that's just peachy, too.

From:	Jules Siegel \<jsiegel@mail.caribe.net.mx\>
To:	pynchon-l@waste.org
Subject:	Rotten attitudes

I'm not any kind of huckster at all. I'm someone who gave up the prospect of fame and fortune because I refused to sell-out my art and my soul. I'm not going to defend myself from this shit. I am not going to argue about who's telling the truth and who's lying. I will say that in my career as a writer I was attacked on many occasions for my political positions, but only once was I ever accused of lying or running a hoax: when my article on Pynchon came out and some idiot who insisted that Pynchon was really J. D. Salinger squawked loudly that I was a hoax.

But really. Making a need known to people who just had a great time with my contributions given freely and without thought of gain. And then to receive this. What a fucking reward. H. L. Mencken once wrote something like, "You can never go wrong underestimating the intelligence of the American public." Well, I say you can never go wrong underestimating the malice of certain people on Pynchon-L.

> *I believe what he actually said was, "No one ever went broke under-estimating the intelligence of the American public."*

Chris Stolz \<chstolz@canuck.com\> wrote:

Siegel, you truly are a pompous self-serving arse. It is good to have a whiff of narcissism on an otherwise thoughtful list. Do you have any claim to fame, or even listenability, other than having had Pynchon bonk your wife way back when?

Jeff Meikle <meikle@mail.utexas.edu> wrote:

Hmmm. What about the following, Jules?

JULES WROTE: *Bianca, obviously, is based on Chrissie, who acted like an eight-year-old with strangers.*

Thought you said you hadn't read GR. Anyway, back on that cosmic Continental road trip, I can just imagine ol' Tom, a haunted look on his face, turning to jive-talkin' younger Tom and gettin' a word in edgewise long enough to ask, rather plaintively, "Who is Jules Siegel and why did he take off with my list?" Maybe Wanda Tinasky's hunched over the public access computer at her local library, greasy carryall at her side, having a high old time now she's discovered how to bypass print and mainline the information superhighway. If this isn't a hoax, is it perhaps a revenger's comedy?

JULES REPLIES: I said that I skimmed it, didn't I? No revenge here. What for? This all took place thirty years or so ago. In the late Sixties and early Seventies, you smoked a joint with another member of your sexual preference and no one else was around.... Just having fun here and getting myself some public attention after fifteen years of total obscurity while living in places where they bring in your luggage on the heads of native bearers (sort of).

davemarc <davemarc@panix.com> wrote:

I hate to break the news to Jules, but former Town of Oyster Bay supervisor Thomas R. Pynchon died of heart failure on July 21, 1995.

From *Newsday*, 7/23/95: "Speaking for my brother," said Judith Pynchon, "I hope that [his success] will not overshadow my father's accomplishments in his long and productive life."

Sometimes I hate getting old, not because it brings me closer to my own death, necessarily, but because more and more news like this arrives, always unexpectedly, always shattering.

JULES REPLIES: This brought tears to my eyes. He was really a great and wonderful man and I cherish every moment that I spent in his company, as few as they were.

Sometimes I hate getting old, not because it brings me closer to my own death, necessarily, but because more and more news like this arrives, always unexpectedly, always shattering.

E.A.Weinstein@qmw.ac.uk wrote:

Pynchonettes Dearly,
(as we hardly need squabble really over such)
Breath. Pynchon. Thomas Pynchon. The fiction of. That which is interesting or valuable in. All together now...lets read a Rainbow...uhhum——
[sorry]
much love,

—E.A.Weinstein
Centre For English Studies
University Of London

---

larsson@vax1.mankato.msus.edu wrote:

When Siegel and others aren't busy ranting at each other, an interesting point emerges from time to time: "He used to do an imitation of Bobby Kennedy singing "Wild Thing" that had Chrissie and I literally rolling on the floor screaming with laughter. Then there were his different ethnic accents. Chrissie is right. Tom could have been an actor. Too bad he was so terrified to appear in public." Hmm. We old-timers might recall the odd hit of someone imitating Senator Everett McKinley Dirksen doing a version of "Wild Thing" (which was sort of inspired by the odd hit record the *real* senator had in "Gallant Men").

Well, the B side of the same record featuring "Wild Thing" by "Senator Everett McKinley" was the same song done by "Senator Bobby" imitating Guess Who? So—was TRP imitating the B side of the record? Was the record imitating TRP? D–did TRP record it *himself*? I've forgotten the name of the original "artist" but I'll bet Dr. Demento fans will know. Any takers?

Don Larsson, Mankato State U (MN)

Henry M <gravity@nicom.com> wrote:

There was a recording of someone imitating a Kennedy (I think John). Oh, yeah. It was Bobby, with a "producer" asking the senator to bear down on the chorus. Ted was on the ocarina.

Could it be just something that was in the air? Did Jules think that TRP had created the lampoon on the spot? Did TRP lead him to think so? Does it matter?

Ahhh, I feel good! I feel the flames dying down. Whew!

I'm ba-ack

To:	pynchon-l@waste.org
From:	Jules Siegel <jsiegel@pdc.caribe.net.mx>
Subject:	*Re:* The Big Heart of Michael Glosup, et al

Those who wish to meet Michael Bigheart's criteria fully, with or without expressing appreciation, can send books to a very deserving friend of mine currently in prison: Joaquin Aldamic c/o Mercedes Sánchez, Domicilio Conocido, Puerto Morelos, Q. Roo

Joaquin is a good and decent father and husband, who wound up on the wrong side of the law and was sent to prison in Chetumal. He became head of the prisoners' internal government in recognition of his intelligence, rectitude and spiritual superiority. After prison protests against prison conditions, a new get-tough warden sent him to Almoloya, the maximum security prison in Mexico City where prisoners of state are held. The prisoners then rioted again in protest.

Anyone who is serious about doing this can send me e-mail and I will get his correct address, as I wouldn't want to burden Mercedes with the cost of re-mailing any books. He will appreciate books in Spanish, but he does read some English.

Following are brief replies to Bigheart's last inane message:

You are presumably employable

I am approximately 50% disabled. I have a plastic hip which was installed twenty years ago and now needs to be replaced. My mobility is quite limited. Despite this, I do work. I just don't earn enough to be able to afford decent books. As you may know, Mexico is going through some very severe economic strains. The peso is very weak. I earn my living in pesos. Books in English are priced in dollars. We have no English-language library.

There are other professional writers on this list, none of whom in my memory have ever dunned us for payment.

Dunning you? Can you read and write, or is Hal the Robot taking dictation here? "…wish to express your appreciation…" = dunning? I said that we would contribute any books we did not want to keep to the *Casa de la Cultura de Cancún.*

I would have to reject you as a worthy candidate for a fund-raiser.

Fund-raiser? What funds? Old books? Old text books for my children?

I happen to fit all of your criteria, except I'm not in custody. Murderers and rapists are more worthy of receiving cast-off books than a writer whose work at one time appeared in publications such as *Esquire, Saturday Evening Post, Best American Short Stories, Best American Magazine Verse*…? My father, however, did spend eight years in special solitary confinement in Danemorra, the New York maximum security prison for incorrigibles. I find your crocodile thanks for the article quite smarmy. Please delete the piece from your hard disk, if you have not done so already. Then report to your nearest mental clinic and ask if they can teach you how to be a human being.

Part 7:
Report Cards & Farewell

It was fun, fun, fun 'til Mommy took the keyboard awaaaay!

I thought some of you might like to receive your report cards so you can use these hours for course credit. Anyone who defended me automatically receives an A+. All not mentioned can apply personally for a rating, which I will post to the list, so watch out!

The following students deserve special mention:

JOHN MASCARO *Anal Aggressive Laureate*—A+
For being a great sport and laughing at his own follies,
but mostly for inspiring the Werewolf.

MICHAEL GLOSUP *Anal Retentive Laureate*—A+
For defining in two short submissions the concept of human asshole.
He made me feel as if I were applying for welfare.

DIANE YORK BLAINE *Class Flirt*—A
Only an A, because I am a sexist.

Doo-Doo Brain Final Awards

First Place

WILL LAYMAN <WILLL@FIELDSCHOOL.COM> WROTE:

Do not, I repeat, do not piss off Jules.
He may call you "doo-doo head."
No I won't, doo-doo brain.

Runner Up

CHRIS STOLZ <CHSTOLZ@CANUCK.COM> WROTE:

*Do you have any claim to fame other
than having had Pynchon bonk your wife way back when?*
Come up with your own insults, doo-doo brain, instead of plagiarizing my
good friend and loyal fan, John Mascaro.

Also Ran

BRUCE APPELBAUM <BRUCE_APPELBAUM@CHEMSYSTEMS.COM> WROTE:

*"...my only claim to fame is that Thomas Pynchon
stopped talking to me in 1968."*
Ibid., doo-doo brain.

FINAL COMMENT: You don't know how this hurts, but the writer always gets the
last word. Mine is *unsubscribe*.

*As it turned out, I did have a few more words to receive and say, as
the conversation now continued for a while by private e-mail with
some of the friends I made while I was on the list. Then, in preparing to put this book together, I looked through the Pynchon-L
Archive and found a few items that either were cute enough or embarrassing enough to publish here.*

Andrew Dinn <andrew@cee.hw.ac.uk> wrote:

*Thanks also for taking the trouble to post your ideas and answer people's questions on
the list.*

It is such an unbelievable pleasure that I want to say "thanks all" in everything
I post. This has been taking up way too much time, however, and I had to face
a very annoyed business partner this morning who has been waiting for about
a week for me to do $ome things that only I can do. I am going to try just to
read the mail and not respond to every interesting blip while I take care of this.
Also, I have been typing so much that the nail on my right forefinger split to

the quick and I can't use the finger. So I think God is telling me to ease off. I'll try, but I feel like a junkie with an unlimited smack connection.

Yeah, that's pretty much what it comes down to.

My supper is ready, so I'll sign off for now. You have my deepest gratitude for the way you've given me encouragement to expose myself in this way. I am not like Tom, but I am not that different from him either. It's just a matter of degree.

Well, it's been an experience, Jules. I'm glad you found the list and found the time to spill a bean or two on Tom. It's also been nice for us to be able to locate the person behind your name and to get a new insight into that decade. Chrissie's input was tantalising, too, if somewhat abbreviated. Thank her very much for her contributions and present our apologies for our part in reviving the awkward corpse of your relationship with her (and also for rattling that skeleton in your once communal cupboard).

---

kyburz@asu.edu wrote:

When reading Pynchon, I always sense some understanding of chaos theory—fractal geometry, etc.

I think that this is what Chrissie was trying to say when she talked about frames. I like holograms better than fractals or chaos theory for this. When you break a hologram you don't get half an image one side and half on another. You get two complete images. As the fragments become smaller, the image loses detail, but it always shows the basic gestalt, until it finally degrades into a kind of whirlpool pattern called a diffraction grid that looks like a galaxy floating in space. The image is contained everywhere on the hologram. I would imagine that fractals and holograms are closely related.

  I interviewed holography pioneer Dennis Gabor, in 1970 for a *Playboy* article on holography. Scientists at Hughes Research showed me a nude female hologram, which I described in the lead. Someone there had a heart attack when a *Playboy* researcher checked the item. Hughes managed to keep the article from ever being published. The editor on the piece later resigned. I like to believe this was a polite way of saying he was discharged, not for incompetence, but because he was a government agent. Corporations tolerate incompetence, not treachery.

BONNIE REPLIED: I guess I don't know too much about holograms. I read your [Pynchon] article; in fact, my creative writing class did too, as we were discussing autobio info and fiction and convergences therein. You were a FAVORITE—excuse me, the Siegel in "Mortality and Mercy" was a favorite with the class—as was the story. So we read more about the alleged man behind the character; rather, we read from him.

From: Hartwin Alfred Gebhardt <hag@iafrica.com>
To: pynchon-l@waste.org
Subject: *Re:* Doo-Doo Brain Final Awards

I seem to have missed a really, like, intense flame war here. I apologize to all affected. All I (sort of) noticed was someone calling someone called Jules Siegel a "fuckwit." I just want to commend Jules Siegel for not lowering himself/herself to that level. "Doo-doo brain" is quite fucking obscene enough. Thank you.

From: kyburz@asu.edu
Subject: Jules
To: pynchon-l@waste.org

Jules wrote one night, frustrated. Maybe you'd like to hear him out. I think he's been unjustly flamed to death. God, it's a bitch to get flamed, isn't it? A-and once it's begun, it's like this monster that feeds on its own disease. I recall jumping right in, ready to flame … anybody! Just let me bitch! I'm not saying we don't often have something to bitch about, but usually, some sense of decency exists among friends, scholars, whatever. Well, you've been preached to death yourselves, I notice, as I've been lurking about lately. So forgive me if Jules' message is timed badly. So, here's what he said:

TOM STANTON WROTE: *[…Early flaming experiences…] My sainted wife finally pointed out […good advice about personal interaction, not always dominating center stage, etc.…]*

Are we married to the same woman? Does Anita have a secret communication going with this woman?

You can imagine what Chrissie went through. Not on the Internet. Right out there with sixty nitballs (nitballs, nutballs, whatever) in the redwoods. She's doing their laundry and cooking their meals, which are mostly paid for by my *Playboy* and *Rolling Stone* expense accounts, and they are attacking us as dilettantes! They were so fucked up they couldn't tie their own shoelaces (not a metaphor, but an actual fact in more than one case). We're exploiting them.

When we split for Mexico the second time in 1973, I once asked her why she hated me: "I married a man in a Brooks Brothers suit who was writing cover stories on major rock stars for magazines like *The Saturday Evening Post*. Mario Puzo, Bruce Jay Friedman and Thomas Pynchon all told me that we were going to be rich and famous because he was going to write best sellers. Now here I am in the jungles of Mexico with a crazy hippie artist and a worried baby. That's why."

Good point.

I was also very touched to read your response about Tom's dad passing, and felt bad that it came across in such a callous way.

I didn't feel Davemarc was callous. How else do you do it? I just fucking hate Wednesdays. The news of my father's death came on a Wednesday. No matter how I try to break the pattern, it's always a dangerous day for me.

As much as this impersonal medium can, your sorrow came through loud and clear.

This is what I do. This is the essence of my art. I make impersonal media wake up singing or crying by putting myself 100% on the line. That's why they call me an egomaniac. That's why they complain about all the self-reflection. Do you want Microsoft Bob talking through the command line? Or do you want a living being? It's a Turing test. It wasn't just the immediate response, it was that you felt you knew me, that there was a connection to another human.

I think the group has gotten very grumpy continually responding to the Werewolf (who was funny) and to being attacked as academics or idiots.

The group? Or individuals who do happen to act like idiots? I didn't say anything negative about academics that I recall. Chrissie made one very apt remark about the sterility of the questions. The flaming is no big deal. It's kind of fun, actually, as the flamers are usually so inept that it's just a matter of letting the thing simmer for a couple of hours until I can figure out the squelch. It's like learning a new program. Dinn must be *insane* at this. Talk about cultural clichés. Does this guy have the clipped British wit down fine? I am studying his technique. The Dancing in the Dark zing to my let it be, let it be: Not on' this list.

I was, however, shocked by the lack of coherence and intelligence, the un-fairness, and the bitterness of some of these responses, the personal attacks, the gratuitous vulgarity and crudeness. I can't imagine what it must be like to be in classrooms or offices with these people. In no way did it upset me person-ally, though.

From Pynchon-L I rarely see the correction or clarification I request. In-stead, there are these tangential flights of free-floating malice based on the authors' personal agendas, not what I wrote.

I'm sorry I don't suffer fools gladly, but if I did I wouldn't have written what some people have worshipped me for over the years. You invite someone like me to your tea party and this is what you get. People wanted to know what we thought of Thomas Pynchon. Now you know. It's not our fault he's not Jesus Christ Superstar. Reading his books, where would you ever get the idea that he was?

I sympathize with the "too much Jules" responses. Sometimes I feel the same way myself. In the present instance, I really was trying to answer the questions. I can't tell you what Thomas Pynchon thought about Cornell and how it formed his writing style. All I can tell you is how I felt about Cornell and allow you to draw inferences. I can't identify his sources. All I can do is describe what Chrissie was like when Tom was writing *Gravity's Rainbow*. Since you are all in the process of a minute study of that book, you can see the correspondences, if any, with what I showed you. I'm not a Barron's Blue Book, nor am I a member of the Thomas Pynchon fan club.

But the book hustle roundhouse did split my face in half. That common criminals were more deserving. The presumption of bad faith. The jealousy of my good fortune. Ignoring the value of the reciprocation I offered. Skipping over the fact that we would donate books we didn't want to a local institution. What a horrible dose of that ignorant American self-righteous Puritanical meddling that I have hated all my life. They just feel they have a God-given right to judge others need and human social value. The Elect. 100% Yankee do-gooder poison.

I work with Javier Murillo, a young Mexican graphic designer who is my business partner. He's really soothing. He pretty much handles the clients. You can imagine my reputation here, but I also have some problems getting around, too. I was so bad today that I couldn't go down to my office—three flights down, too much of a walk—because I had been up most of the night just seething, so Javier came up and found me on the bed waiting for Anita to finish making lunch. I told him what was bothering me. He said in Spanish, "Just fuck those people. Remember who you are. Tell them you don't want any fucking books, that you've got plenty of dough, you'll buy your own. How much do you need for these books? I'll get Roberto [his rich friend] to get them for you."

I said, "Never. I just laid out where I was at to them. I'm not ashamed. Let them feel ashamed."

It was just the whole sickness of America pouring through my heart. People have been really good to us here, except for the occasional business maggot. Anita and I have watched no more than a few hours of television a year since we met in 1977, and not much more in the years before that. It's been fifteen years since I had direct contact with anything like that.

> *This is very important to understand in considering why I got so angry. I am of an earlier generation than Pynchon-L. I'm hardly an old fogey, but I would never have dared to express myself to an elder in the way some of the list members did. No young Mexican would ever treat anyone my age in such a disrespectful manner. Americans are quite boorish by Mexican standards, especially in the way we treat our elders. On the Internet one's identity tends to blur, but at this point in the interaction, most list members were well aware of my age and accomplishments. Unfortunately, familiarity does breed contempt.*

Bonnie Kyburz <kyburz@asu.edu> wrote: *Can you explain the dearth of books?*

The Hotel Zone sells only awful trashy thrillers and romance paperbacks at absurd prices. Cancun itself is a post-revolutionary development in a post-revolutionary society. Print is superfluous. They come in from some remote Yucatecan town with a palm-thatch school room and they go directly to com-

'Your book hustle lampoon was quite funny.'

puter school. Books don't like the humidity, either. Cockroaches eat the paper and the glue.

This is the Third World. Underdevelopment applies to information as well. There are hardly any libraries here and the only English books they do have are those left in hotel rooms and then donated by the hotels. I can't afford to buy books by mail. So we are just going crazy for lack of reading material that doesn't talk back disrespectfully and unexpectedly bring news that yet another revered elder has fallen.

Try to understand my situation this way: suppose Tom Stanton looked into the Velikovsky thing and came away convinced that this was all an unfortunate tragedy, that the man had some serious questions to ask about the conventional time-line. Then he started talking about this and tried to get it published in *National Geographic*. When this failed, he went public and told the whole story in other media—including mordant observations about why the editors scorned his desire to give Velikovsky a fair hearing.

How long would he last at *National Geographic*? Could he then go to work at *Smithsonian*?

I wrote about cutting edge social and political issues. I made important hidden enemies. Because of my political connections and the general esteem in which I was held by young, influential editors (whose careers were advanced by the response to my work during a major prolonged thaw), I was given even more liberty to speak out clearly in defense of reformist ideas that threatened the existing class structure.

To Pynchon readers, "They" are, perhaps, a literary metaphor. Not to me.

Understand why I can't afford books and why I asked people not to put anything odd in my mail? I would never compromise Pynchon's personal security by revealing his address, if I knew it. That part I understand very well. I just feel I have no obligation to protect his image as well.

Meanwhile, thanks for the comforting remarks. I feel very blue today. The news about Tom's father was like a skeleton tap on the shoulder, coming in the middle like that. Despite my tolerant remarks, I think flaming is infantile bullshit. These people are uncivilized boobs. I think that sort of thing should be squashed on the Internet by the sheer force of fully expressed social disapproval, even if some would consider this repressive. Never mind PC. Let's just have some common courtesy.

Tonight is the eve of *Día de Los Muertos*. You're supposed to honor the faithful dead and make jokes about death. I'll try.

As always,

—Jules

From:	mglosup@randomc.com
To:	Kyburz@asu.edu
Subject:	*Re:* Jules
cc:	jsiegel@pdn.caribe.net.mx,
	pynchon-l@waste.org

JULES SIEGEL WROTE: *But the book hustle roundhouse did split my face in half.*

This was not my intention at all.

That common criminals were more deserving.

I never stated "common criminals" were more deserving than you. There are a lot of people involved with the American criminal justice system who are less than criminal. But in any case I wasn't implying that serial murderers and child molesters should be considered over you.

The presumption of bad faith.

I didn't presume bad faith on your part. I thought your "book hustle" lampoon was quite funny. I never thought that your request was a scam, just a tacky addendum to what I perceived as a pattern of obnoxiousness. And now I'm rethinking that judgment—the tacky addendum part anyway.

The jealousy of my good fortune.

Not an issue.

Ignoring the value of the reciprocation I offered.

Now we're getting somewhere, as in the part where you are correct. I devalued your efforts. You gave freely of your time and your work and I should have thanked you instead of snidely denouncing you.

Skipping over the fact that we would donate books we didn't want to a local institution.

Guilty. I conveniently, unjustifiably ignored this originally.

What a horrible dose of that ignorant American self-righteous Puritanical meddling that I have hated all my life. They just feel they have a God-given right to judge others need and human social value. The Elect. 100% Yankee do-gooder poison.

I resemble that remark.

I sincerely apologize to you, Jules, for discounting your needs, but especially for misrepresenting your appeal. Before I wrote this response, I reread your comments accompanying your posting of the *Playboy* article. My response is very different for having done so.

You quite graciously requested that anyone wishing to show their appreciation do so by helping you obtain quality reading material, which is a difficult task in your circumstances. In the context of those long ago times and in the context of the sum of your postings, I read it differently. I hope you accept this as non-crocodilian remorse for undeserved attacks I made on you and gratitude for your generosity of time and effort.

I also apologize to the list for any s/n ratio fluctuations you may have experienced. Resume flaming on other fronts.
                    —Michael Glosup

JULES: Turn in your Laurels, Glosup. You will now receive an Award of Merit for Service to Humanity.

From:	willl@fieldschool.com
Subject:	Sincere response
To:	Jules Siegel

Dear Jules—

It has certainly been exciting to see the great tumult caused by your intersection with the ol' Pynchon Mailing List. I think that you were onto something when you pointed out, in one post or another, that the list seemed unable to enjoy sarcasm, irony or just plain old jokin' around—that many members of the list seemed thin-skinned and too protective of Thomas Pynchon as some kind of literary deity. I enjoyed reading your posts and feel no peculiar embarrassment at enjoying knowledge of some personal details of Pynchon. (My question, had I bothered to ask one, would have been to find out the actual degree of knowledge and interest Pynchon had about jazz, my own strong interest.)

JULES REPLIES: He was deeply interested in jazz when I knew him. All I know about this is the Thelonious Monk anecdote in my article.

WILL: I admit that I love his books (why else would I be a member of this list?) and that I hold him in some awe for his ability to create books that I consider so genuinely profound. But I'm not in awe of him as a person (how could I be?), nor do I feel that I would be disappointed to learn that he was less than a paragon. Because of all that, I welcomed your presence on the list both because I enjoyed learning about Pynchon and because it seemed valuable and interesting for the list to be shaken up a bit.

Perhaps there have been privately communicated personal attacks on you, ones I'm not privy to, that got ugly. But—in the spirit of being loose and not-too-thin-skinned, you seemed to be laughing off the barbs of the list, doing your Werewolf thing, whatever. My reaction was, I suppose, one of continuing amusement. I hadn't been part of the discussion, of course, but it still seemed harmless and interesting—a nice contrast to the frequently boring academic chit-chat of the list.

My sarcastic post about your reference to someone as a "doo-doo head" was intended to convey my sense that the list's discussion with you had become juvenile and *ad hominem*—on both sides but, in my opinion, particularly from you. My impression is that you were alternating between two modes of expression: a very logical, intellectual style that dissected people's opinions point-by-point, and the kind of smarty-pants attacks epitomized by

Uh-oh. Is the list turning into a Leo Buscaglia hug-fest?

your Pampers theme—demeaning and hurtful on the one hand, but also having the quality of being deliberately bad in the manner of kid making fart noises in English class—perhaps still disrupting but doing so to lighten everybody up.

JULES: Excellent analysis. Is there any chance you could be talked into writing a dissertation on me? I was pointing out the infantile and anally aggressive nature of Mascaro's stubbornness. He said he was going to continue to be slovenly and imprecise in his postings despite my earlier logical, intellectual request that he think things through before sending out ill-considered attacks.

WILL: Because of this impression of you and your role here on the list, I am quite surprised to find you—the fart-making Werewolf, if you will—so upset at the joking around at your own expense, particularly my ambiguous one-liner that earned my first prize in the Doo-Doo Brain sweepstakes. Or, perhaps, was this still light-hearted kidding on your part?

JULES: I think you should check the battery in your humor implant. Yes, it was very light hearted kidding.

WILL: I'm writing you now because I am sincerely unhappy if, intentionally or not, I've upset anyone. On the other hand, I think you ought to understand that the reaction of at least this one person to you was mixed. You conveyed a very strong sense of sincerity at one moment and then a cavalier fuck-'em-if-they-can't-take-a-joke attitude the next moment. Your hurt "unsubscribe" message today makes me wonder which attitude is the pose and which is real—or if they…these two Juleses…are running around together.
     In any case, sorry if I pissed you off, but on the other hand … .
          —Will Layman

JULES: The unsubscribe was not in any way hurt. That was your projection based on the modest guilt feelings you express here. I was quite angry at Michael Golsup for his nasty book attack, but other than that I enjoyed the entire experience.
     Thanks for taking the time to write me such a thoughtful letter.

Henry M <gravity@nicom.com> wrote:

Uh-oh. Is The List turning into a Leo Buscaglia hug-fest?

But seriously, it's good to see people able to apologize, "sorry seems to be the hardest word."

| *From:* | Kyburz@ASU.Edu |
| *To:* | Jules Siegel <jsiegel@pdc.caribe.net.mx> |

Jules—here's a nice reply from Andrew:

Andrew Dinn <andrew@cee.hw.ac.uk> wrote:

Bonnie,

Thanks for posting Jules' note. I think much of the difficulty Jules encountered was due to a generation gap—sorry to revive that cliché but it is so appropriate. For example, Jules said to me he felt that maybe he had not done a very good job as a provider for his family. *Provider???* A very old-fashioned term, to my ear, and not one I could ever conceive of using with regard to my life. Ditto Jules comments *re* his "beautiful wife." I know that what he means is to convey his pride in her and admiration for her, a sense of wonder and of being blessed to be married to her. Only I have to bend my ear to be able to hear that beneath his phrasing.

—Andrew Dinn

To:	<mascaro@humnet.ucla.edu>
From:	Jules Siegel <jsiegel@mail.caribe.net.mx>
Subject:	Keep in touch

Dear John,

I didn't get a chance until now to answer your mostly conciliatory message, which I am sorry I did not read more carefully before replying publicly. I was really enraged by Glosup. I hate to reveal my economic or physical situation, because I don't want to look as if I'm playing the victim to earn sympathy, but I finally had to just go ahead and expose myself in order to deal with this. His

Psychoanalysis is not going to help a motherless child

letters reminded me of the scene in Brett Easton Ellis's psycho book (if I have the author's name right) in which the affluent killer lectures his skid row victim about getting a job and becoming a useful member of society. Glosup's was the only message in the whole series that got me angry. The news of Tom's father's death didn't help much either. I wasn't at my best there, not that my best is very forbearing.

Hey, that Pampers thing, wow, am I cut or what?

You are probably putting them on too tight. Also, there are different sizes.

It was fun jousting with you, John. I'm not putting Tom down for his drug use. It's not all that much of what I did write about him. The section that got you ticked off really was not about drugs, but an attempt to communicate the states of mind I was talking about by comparing the effects of amphetamine (which I believe most writers and students have taken and therefore will recognize) and stress hormones. He was a doper. So was I. Why was I supposed to ignore that?

If you look at the piece with a fresh eye, you'll see that what I was saying is that I feel Tom suffered from severe chronic anxiety, which is reflected in the super-sensitivity bordering on paranoia in his personal lifestyle, as well as in what his reviewers call the lapidary effect of his writing. Over-elaboration of detail is not a judgmental description. I use it instead of lapidary, because his writing doesn't seem to me to be polished as much as very carefully worked. Have you ever considered the comforting function of clutter?

I appreciate your points about doper politics. Yet I don't feel I have any reason to not discuss drug use, whether positively or negatively, in order to protect anyone's political position or literary image. Drugs are good and drugs are bad. There are good drugs and bad drugs. There are good drug users and bad drug users. Without wanting to seem to criticize you personally, I do have to say that I find any politically-imposed restrictions on free inquiry and expression to be quite Stalinistic. Political correctness is just another form of liberal Stalinism. I say encourage truth, plain speaking, good humor and simple human courtesy.

[...too much Jules...]

As I was very careful to state, my only special knowledge about him is limited to his early publishing and writing years. The reason I'm so prominent in the picture I draw is not that I'm an egomaniac (although I certainly am), but because I really am trying to give the Pynchon list a picture of the time and the influences as I saw them. I have no idea how Tom saw them. You say you're about my age—61?—but most of the questions I saw were from kids who have no idea what the Sixties and early Seventies were like. Now they can take the testimony of an eyewitness and apply it to their study of Pynchon's earlier work.

This may sound egotistical beyond mania, but I don't have to promote my persona. The texture of my writing speaks for itself. I don't believe a writer can present an objective reality. He can only write what he saw and felt. You look at a television screen and you see all these little people, but what you mostly see, in terms of sheer visual mass, is the television set itself. That's me in my writing. Who is it who is seeing and reporting?

I stand on the comments about Hunter S. Thompson.

I never liked his politics or his writing style either. I have no absolute position on drug use, but I do feel it is unwise to encourage chemical drug gluttony, because it will have serious effects on the liver and the immune system. You wouldn't put benzene up your nose. Nor might you use black market cocaine if you saw how it was made. Are you aware of Peter Duesberg's position on excessive chemical abuse causing AIDS, which is attacked on similar grounds as yours, although they don't dare come out and say it? What if all these chemical drugs, not HIV, really are a primary cause of AIDS, just as Duesberg claims? Do we ignore this because drugs are politically sacrosanct in certain intellectual circles? Or because malnutrition, poverty and the depressing effects of heteronomy (see, I can use these terms, too) are equally important in the AIDS picture?

I am one of those old-fashioned hippies who believe that drugs are a sacrament, not another version of booze. Taking LSD and the other psychedelics saved my life. Amphetamine almost ended it. I'm in chronic pain a lot of the time now and I don't know how I would have gotten through this far without grass. I thought of suicide often in the past few years just to escape the hell of being physically handicapped like this, never mind the pain itself. Walking used to be my favorite recreation. I'm not a shut-in, but pretty close. I don't want to die of liver or kidney disease, so I have to limit my use of pain-killers drastically. Fortunately, last year someone gave me a book on the psychology of chronic pain, and I have been able to get surprisingly consistent relief through breathing methods and understanding what emotional factors trigger my worst pain episodes.

Politically, I am the American version of a Social Democrat, not a Libertarian. We're real serious folk. I used to write about politics from the standpoint of sociology and psychology—why strict constructionists are best explained by strict toilet training, for example. Psychoanalysis is useful for this, but it's very limiting. The effects themselves are actually more behavioral. Psychoanalysis does provide a convenient map and diagnostic labels. The theory is not very convincing, however.

All the psychoanalysis in the universe is not going to help a motherless child—and that's what we all are, really, motherless children. I urge you to look into case histories of mass murderers and see the common thread of childhood neglect and abuse. I am against the NOW-style feminists because they embraced business culture. Children were 14 on NOW's priority lists before I left the United States in 1981. How do you think you would have felt as a child if you knew that you were 14 on your mother's list of 15?

I am in favor of an industrial policy that will lead to a stable economy—with a big environmental clean-up as the keystone of a domestic Marshall Plan. I think all drug use should be decriminalized and marijuana should be made legal, but forbidden to exploitation by corporations or limited partnerships. Individuals and partnerships will then be personally liable for any damages. This will keep them from putting additives in it, for example, which are suspected to be principal agents in the carcinogenic effects of tobacco, and will generally tend to enforce a certain kind of Darwinian responsibility. No one wants to be the loser of the next asbestos-type lawsuit.

Cocaine is a very tough call. I would make the leaves generally available, as I feel that most people in the cities use cocaine for the same reason they do in the Andes, to increase the uptake of oxygen to the brain and overcome the effects of smog. People do have a right to breathe, but it's sad to see them blasting their brains with dubiously adulterated koo-koo powders when a pleasant tea would do the job without the horrible side effects.

Please drop me a line when you've had a chance to reflect on these thoughts—but try to leave out the vitriol. It's not necessary. If you're interested in communicating with me (and I would welcome your thoughts) maybe it will be better if you don't try to do it all at once. Pick a single point and elaborate on that, keeping in mind the context I'm trying to lay out here.

> *John wrote back in a truly gentlemanly and funny manner, but I've lost the original text, except for my reply. The best moment for me in his note was when he ruefully went along with the Pampers gag and said that he had tried the larger ones and they were much more comfortable. John also wrote that he knew there was a guy he could like under all that defensive posturing—but he wasn't sure if that guy were him or I. I replied:*

Great line. I was going to say don't be too sure that it's either of us. I just loved bopping those dopes with a ball peen hammer. Murthy wrote me a note apologizing for things "getting off on a wrong foot." Anita and I had to laugh at this. It's just me. Anytime I open my mouth in public, some people will immediately go into cardiac arrest and then begin screaming at me and each other, while others titter and burst into peals of laughter.

> *Just as I was about to send off this final main text to Dale L. Larson, I received the following communication from Andrew Dinn.*

Andrew Dinn <andrew@cee.hw.ac.uk> wrote:

I was reading Tony Tanner's book on Pynchon this weekend, in particular his comments on "Mercy and Mortality in Vienna" and its "hero," Cleanth Siegel, who walks out on the chance to become a saviour. And I thought that whoever suggested Cleanth was you got it all totally wrong. I think you would probably have jumped straight away at the chance to save at least some small part of the world, much to your own credit *and* personal distress. Whereas, Cleanth is just another version of Tom, abdicating responsibility, in fact running like hell to get away from it. I have a lot of respect for your sense of duty, although personally I am frequently tempted to do a Tom. And in response, rather than answer the call to self-crucifixion, I merely force myself to attend to chipping away at my own, my friends' and my acquaintances' need for salvation. So, Jules, there's a vote of confidence and affection just when you least expected it. I'll stop now before I get too maudlin.

JULES: This is very flattering, but your note actually finally makes me understand what Chrissie was saying when she told me that I was Cleanth Siegel. That's how I was when Tom knew me. I'd say that until I met Chrissie I never had the slightest jot of feeling for another person, much less Humanity. Chrissie was and is a truly loving person who taught me the value of compassion. I was just too scarred by my life to appreciate this. She is an engulfing lover. I was always more like Laurence Harvey in "Room at the Top" or "The Manchurian Candidate." He came from the same stock as I did, Lithuanian Jew, very dry and cold culturally, suspicious of ecstasy.

Chrissie is really third-generation Irish, although her father was Old Settler French-German stock, hence her name, Jolly, originally Jolie. Her mother and her aunts all still spoke with slight Irish accents when I met them and her grandmother had an Irish brogue tempered with New York. When Chrissie was in a good mood, she used to go around singing, "Ireland was Ireland when England was a pup. Ireland will be Ireland when England's gobbled up." Her grandmother said as a young girl, "I'll marry an Englishman and torture him to death." She wasn't joking. So Chrissie was deeply mystical and devoted to Passion, but cunning. She used to call me Mishkin because she thought I was exactly like the character in Doestoevsky's *The Idiot*. I refused to read the book for fear of finding out what this meant. Anita, whose family is mostly still culturally Old Settler Huguenot French, understands me much better than Chrissie ever could, because she was raised in the same dry, cold way that I was.

ANDREW: Chrissie sounds like an utter peach.

JULES: Not exactly.

> *I thought that would have been the end, but all was still not finished. Earlier, when I had queried John about his missing letter, he at first sent me another really great letter offering his congratulations and magnanimously volunteering his permission to publish our exchanges. Technically, I didn't need his permission, as the material falls very clearly under the concept of fair use, but as a courtesy, I*

had Dale send him the proofs of Lineland, *thinking he might like to edit his posts a little or write some commentary at the end.*

Oh my.

Electronic messages do have a different effect than the printed word, no doubt about that. John saw himself frozen in his own write and had a few second thoughts. A few. By now you know John Mascaro almost as well as you know me, so you can use your imagination and picture the e-mail messages burning the wires across continents and oceans. But John is a great guy, after all, and after some forceful encouragement from Andrew Dinn and a lot of smoothing over by Dale L. Larson and a bit of the usual Jules Siegel machine-gun trouble-making verbal stingray, he made a few minor changes and wrote the following short essay. If anyone ever doubted the ability of the book to survive any assault by any other medium, I think John's thoughts will put those fears to rest forever.

Between the Lines of *Lineland*

By JOHN MASCARO

I HAVE COME TO BE IN A BOOK I hadn't really wanted to be in. How this odd and unanticipated turn of events befell me might be one of the themes of this book, the one you are now reading. When Jules Seigel [*sic*—grrr!] showed up on the Pynchon List, I was one of the first, though not the last, to get into an exchange with him that quickly reached flash point. I hadn't intended that, but it was part of the learning experience laid out here. The arc of our little flame war soon peaked and settled earthward as Jules and I smoothed over our quarrel in a few private posts. Soon afterward Jules retired from active participation (after giving "grades" to everyone he'd tangled with), and that, I assumed, was that. So I was surprised when he posted me a few months later that he'd written a book based on his brief experience with the p-list, and that I was a big part of this book. I was happy for Jules, since I knew how badly he wanted to come back to life as a writer, and it seemed clear from his message that he felt he'd done so.

Things soon got more complicated, though, as Jules explained a little more of what was actually in the book. When I finally received a galley of the book, I wasn't sure how I felt about being in it, and after a few days I told Jules I'd prefer not to. That's when I learned a little more about Jules than I had during our fight and reconciliation. I also learned more about writing in cyberspace, and about how words I never even thought of as having a fully real existence not only did so, but had acquired a new level of reality, a hyperreal existence. They were still "mine" (I owned them; I still do, I think) but no longer mine alone. They floated out there, dancing like electrons, waiting for anybody who felt like snaring them and redirecting them. And that's what Jules planned to do, and my demurral wasn't going to stop him.

Jules has assumed that my request to be left out of *Lineland* stemmed from a reluctance to see our fight—or at least my contributions to it—aired publically. It is true that my posts sound to me a little like listening to fingernails screech on a blackboard. It seems impossible that the tones they strike are mine, since they are so far off from what I thought I was writing. Not their literal meanings, but their context has changed, and that changes everything. And when words whose writer assumed were off on some comet loop, never to return in this lifetime at least, reappear as though from the phantom zone, in a new context but wearing the same gossamer-thin semantic veils, they seem almost indecently exposed. Print is real, it has weight and takes up space (feel the book in your hand); e-mail is just disembodied chat. But of course that's just my essentially old fashioned, if not Luddite, view.

This said, it's not the real reason I asked to pass on *Lineland*. Those objections are a little more complex. But since the book is real, and here, let us say my objections are a moot, or perhaps a still open, question. Actually, they are pretty clearly laid out, or at least prefigured, in the ways Jules and I clash here, each defending his side. That's probably fair enough for a reader to work through. And also to judge whether or not the ephemera of words launched into air, meant to melt, ambushed in the ether and redeployed, can form, when transmuted by craft and will, the all too solid flesh of a book.

—Los Angeles, April 3, 1997

Seeing yourself in print is like being in one of those dreams where you are naked in the wrong place. No matter how carefully you manufacture your image, the real you always emerges. "Would some giftie, the giftie gie us, to see ourselves as others see us," wrote John Burns. Chrissie always said, "Be careful what you wish. You might get it." Well, the wish is there and it seems impossible to evade. One of my most affectionate reviewers, Patricia Bosworth, said that I write to stay sane. But sanity has its cost and the prime cost is the shattering of the pathetic little ego mirror under the hammer of the press.

There's a great deal of hand-wringing going on in some literary circles. People are already beginning to mourn the passing of the old card catalog as the computer terminal takes over from the faded cards and old blonde oak cases. I've thought about these questions and I've come up with some answers, which I think really do belong at the end of a book like this. As Yogi Berra said, "It ain't over 'til it's over." When the author is running the show, when is it ever over?

The Future *of the* Book
of the Future

NOT LONG AGO, I received a flyer from Franklin Furnace Archive requesting submissions for a new show to be called "The Future of the Book of the Future" inspired in part, I'm sure, by the electronic books debate. With the advent of the CD-ROM disc and other book-like devices, doubts have been aroused that the conventional book can survive at all. This is rather like the debate that followed the introduction of photography by Daguerre, a French portrait artist who invented silver plate photography in order to make portrait painting easier, just as Dürer before him used the *camera obscura* and the coordinate grid system to solve certain problems of perspective, thereby laying the ground for both Daguerre and Descartes. As we have seen, painting did survive photography very well. Photography itself then began the struggle to be accepted as a fine art, while painters scrambled to define themselves as more than mere illustrators, leading to such decidedly non-realistic genres as abstract impressionism and, ultimately, performance art, which defies both realism and Descartes.

The fraud of fine art vs. commercial art

The well-used cliché complains that our best poets and writers are working for advertising agencies. More interesting, and less obvious, is the fact that so are our best graphic designers and illustrators. Now what about people like me, who combine all these skills to create the most humble and yet most significant art of our time, the concrete poetry that has no name, but forms the visual and editorial tapestry that rules our lives?

Dürer was a commercial artist who worked for printers. Fine art is great art only by definition and the definitions are set down by people who do not have to justify their decisions even to each other. That's why so much of it is ugly and obscure. The greatness of commercial art is defined by its utility. This

To assert absolute control, the curator had to castrate realism.

grounds it in a kind of bedrock reality imposed by traditions of a visual grammar that goes back to the monuments of antiquity.

The world of fine art holds realism in such contempt because realism is too dangerous. It is instantly accessible by all classes of society. It has content. It can carry opinions. It can put a sneer on an image that forever turns the viewer against the idea it represents. Realism has its own set of values, which cannot be changed by mere definition and therefore are beyond the control of people who can decide on their own whim whether or not, say, a given work of performance art is Art or *dreck*. To assert absolute control over art, the curator had to castrate realism. This was done without mercy with the most economical of weapons, the raised eyebrow. N. W. Wyeth was dismissed as a mere illustrator and it drove him insane and ruined his life. I personally find him to have been a much greater artist than the "fine" Wyeths who followed, who are not quite his equal as technicians, and much his inferior in emotion.

Ugliness seems to prove seriousness and worth, as in feminist theory. Serious people are plain and wear thick glasses with thin tortoise-shell frames. It's the same with art. It must be nervous and bony or it is kitsch. The serious writer must fit certain Literature 101 parameters: symbolism, things to footnote, grist for the eventual Variorum edition. Clarity is pandering to the masses. I say *pander*.

The corporate world embraced Abstract Impressionism because it went with any decor, had no political meaning, yet was fashionably progressive and even revolutionary. The value of this kind of meaningless art was established by political commissars called museum curators, whose salaries were paid by the corporate state, and could raise an artist from abject poverty to wealth by absolute fiat alone. It's really quite diabolical, when you think about it. All artists are politically dangerous. By dividing art into fine art and commercial art you effectively control the two most important groups of artists. The commercial artists are, by definition, sold out to the machine, and therefore firmly under control. The serious artist has been brought under the economic control of the fine art system. That was the overt lesson of the NEA controversies. It's all kind of like Midnight Basketball. You like to know where your artists are, and the best way to do that is to set out the feeding troughs.

The book as object

I am already creating futuristic books, but they don't look at all like Buck Rogers. They look like eminently traditional books, even a little old-fashioned. But each book is a one-of-a-kind production. I make each one myself on my laser printer with color pages printed on an excellent ink jet printer. Then I bind them myself. Each copy of a given title is different from every other:

- The text and illustrations are in constant process, as I add to the book and make corrections.

- Each binding is different, although they do resemble each other as I work with a favorite set of materials. Right now, I'm using *papel amate*, a kind of Mexican papyrus made from the bark of a local variety of *ficus*.

- Each book is endorsed with the name of the patron and date of creation set in type as a running footer. A technical description documents the specifics of the book's individuality.

Books will branch into two distinct forms:

The electronic book will be at a disadvantage until the emergence of a distinctly book-like hand-held viewing device at about the price of a decent transistor radio, but with much greater visual and aesthetic standards than current state-of-the-art notebook and sub-notebook computers. The "page" will have to be rock-solid and have very high resolution.

The technology already exists to do this, and a bit of study will predict the time of arrival. Until this device is in mass production, however, electronic books will be mainly useful for disseminating large amounts of information in searchable form, rather than novels, biographies and other "reader" books, as the current computer screen does not lend itself to sustained reading.

One important exception will be poetry, which will merge with multi-media and will include voice, illustrations, music and visuals. Eventually, the electronic book will become the preferred mass medium, and will resemble television as it relies more and more on multi-media effects. As long as it continues to have pages, it will be a book.

The traditional book will always survive, just as calligraphic manuscripts do for sacred objects, such as the hand-lettered Hebrew Torah, but books will take on more and more of the market characteristics of art objects. The important word here is "possession." People like books as objects, not only to have and hold, but also to display. Electronic media are unlikely ever to supplant books as permanent objects. A well-made book is essentially timeless, but an electro-magnetic computer disk is guaranteed for only five years and then begins to deteriorate. Optical media (such as CD-ROM) have much longer lives, but all electronic media are subject to the vagaries of the output device. Phonograph records become increasingly difficult to use with age, not only because they wear out, but also because the player becomes technologically extinct. When the last wire recorder dies, how do you read all those wires?

Books in general will be shaped by the computer in ways that are not likely to be very well understood by non-writers. Book art tends to look at the book as a visual, concrete object and to ignore the experience of creating and read-ing text. This does lead to many interesting and valuable creative insights, but the most important part of the book as an experience will always be the text. Pictures and illustrations are wonderful, but nothing engages you like reading a good book, because it creates a kind of hypnotic state in which you enter the book and become a part of the world it creates. Your mind supplies the sensual environment, as it does in a dream.

You don't want the reader to stop and notice the beauty of your writing too often, but to be swept along on a river of sensation. For most writers, the hardest part of the work is the constant revision. You change a word here and then you have to change Lord knows how many other words on different pages. Something as simple as changing a character's name means hours of work if you are using a typewriter or writing the book out by hand. The computer makes this part much easier.

Kirkpatrick Sale dramatically smashed a computer in Carnegie Hall to pub-licize his book on the Luddites. If only there were a way of publishing a book without the word processor, he whined in *Wired*. How can anyone be such a *schmuck* as to attack the word processor? Talk about a miracle of modern tech-nology that relieves anxiety better than two Valium! The computer has hu-manized the worst parts of the publishing process, principally in the area of typesetting. Hot metal Monotype is still the most beautiful typography, but no one mourns the passing of Linotype and Ludlow. Lead is poisonous. It's heavy.

Try lifting a chase. Hot metal is dangerous, as I found out once when a Linotype machine began spitting exploding molten type metal at me.

Although Sales and his ilk perceive the computer to be a force for control (which it certainly is), it is a much greater force of liberation, putting an important tool of production directly in the hands of the worker—and the dissident, as the Russians found out during the collapse of the Communist system, when computer techies ran circles around old-line officials, as they did during the recent election protests in Serbia.

Ultimately the key word in the future of the future of the book is freedom. Electronic media and the computer will free artists and writers to communicate in new ways that will not make sense until we actually see them. One not very far-out idea: a three-dimensional book in the form of a displayable hologram, with pages that turn and have depth, as well as movement. Add the dimension of time and interactivity and this book begins to take on the characteristics of a living being, lacking only self-consciousness.

To the animist, all things are alive. Electronic media have highly animistic qualities and people who work in them have value systems and beliefs that closely parallel those of traditional animism. Thus these new forms of books will tend to encourage the evolution of new forms of religion and ethical systems with unpredictable changes in human behavior. Anyone who has played the computer game Doom knows how effective it is in harmlessly discharging aggression. War and individual violence will go the way of human sacrifice, replaced by computer simulations as first the bull fight and then the football game replaced the gladiators of the Roman Circus, and Jesus Christ replaced the ritual killing of sacrificial victims to assure fertility.

Almost thirty years ago, *Playboy* sent me to do a story on computer simulation. At the IBM Educational Center in San Jose, California, I played chess with a computer that printed out the moves on a line printer. Some months later, in New York, I realized that the computer printer of the future would be similar to a Xerox machine, rather than an impact printer.

Computer typography was then quite ugly because of the rather primitive programming of the time and the optical compromises necessary to convert to film designs originally cut in metal. This ugly type triumphed and drove the craftsmanship and the craftsmen out of the marketplace. Type could now be set by non-union help from the typing pool at four dollars an hour. Metal type became too expensive for me to use.

I became very sad. My medium was dying and with it the friendship and camaraderie of the great artists and technicians who had so often made my life and career seem worthy even when I was creating trivial (and sometimes malicious) propaganda. They were my audience, for only they could appreciate the quality of my work. The essence of great typography is invisibility. A great work of typographic design looks inevitable. It has a fundamental simplicity that requires a lapidary attention to detail and polish. How many people have the kind of vision required to appreciate the invisible?

Today, the computer that I fantasized is sold in Sears. It is a very exciting time for artists such as myself. At my local newsstand here in the Cancun Hotel Zone, I can buy slick color magazines that discuss in minute detail the most refined and esoteric aspects of my art. But the camaraderie of the old hot metal type shop hardly exists any more. The typographer works alone now. I am weeping openly as I write these words. It was hard, industrial work, and it required men with great forearms who could lift heavy metal chases. I never lifted a chase, but I respected those who did. They taught me the meaning of economy and dignity. Some of the happiest moments of my life were spent in those shops. The computer and the laser printer have given me once again the medium I thought had died. It is a new thing to work alone in this way. One does not weep in the print shop. Perhaps we have lost some of the joy, but the tears may be more important.

A few months ago, I sent the query to Dale L. Larson that he mentions in his Preface. In February, he showed up here in Cancun and we worked out the final details of *Lineland: Mortality and Mercy on the Internet's Pynchon-L Discussion List*. In the most unlikely manner, at a time when I least expected it, my childhood wish to create my own books—my own in every detail—was about to be realized. The most difficult struggle in my development as an artist has been to give up the desire to be published by Knopf and reviewed in *The New York Times*. It is still quite a struggle, but this book shows why it has been well worth the effort. There will be more to come.

—CANCUN, QUINTANA ROO, MEXICO
March 24, 1997, 6:02 AM, Full Moon in Libra

Frequently Asked Questions

As you tour the Internet, you'll find pages called FAQs, a TLA standing for Frequently Asked Questions, which, I hope, is self-explanatory. My FAQs draw many compliments, as does my online resumé in general. Because it's referred to more than once in the text, Dale L. Larson asked me to put it in the book in full, but I think you now know enough about me to last more than one lifetime, so I'm just giving you the good parts, including the photographs, which he found more than worthy of your attention.

Why are you showing us these naked pictures of your wife? Don't you realize that this will cut down on your job offers?

No one that stupid is going to offer me a job anyway. The idea is to get your attention and demonstrate my talent.

Why doesn't she call herself Anita Siegel?

It's bad enough that I have to be called Jules Siegel. If I didn't have so much invested in him, I would call myself Mr. Anita Brown.

What about your children's names? Faera Siegel Jolly? Eli Siegel Brown? Jesse Siegel Brown?

This is a Mexican custom. Faera's mother was Chrissie Jolly. Isn't it nice for children to have both parents' names? Besides, it makes it easier to sort out the fruits of the various marriages we all have.

Are you a marijuana-smoking hippie who moved to Mexico for grass and cheap tequila?

As difficult as it might be to believe, this is an actual verbatim question I received. Grass is very illegal in Mexico, although I have heard there are people who have been known to do illegal things even in Cancun. Tequila is not always cheap. I saw one bottle for $300 when I did a menu for one of Faera's clients. I was enough of a hippie to have written a major piece about communes for *Playboy* and I actually lived in a commune in Marin County for

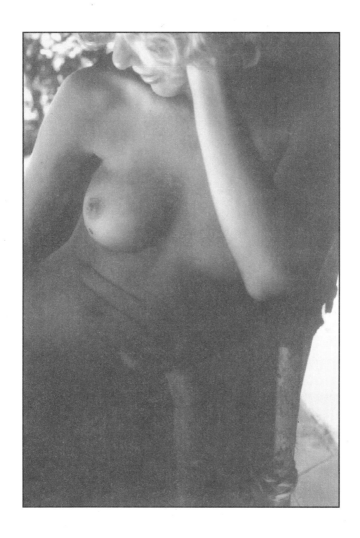

ANITA BROWN
Yelapa, Jalisco, 1977
Photograph by Jules Siegel

almost two years while covering a war between dope dealers for *Rolling Stone*. Not that I ever inhaled myself, of course. [This cliché is now mandatory.] Probably that's why Wenner rejected the story.

Turned out he had been bought into by Max Palevsky (big Xerox investor) and was now a good little businessman (his word—proudly, in an editorial) and he wanted a hatchet job on evil dope dealers.

These guys weren't evil (although some of them were real bad). Some were actually quite heroic in their dedication to feeding and caring for people who would otherwise have been in mental institutions or on the streets. I fed a few myself. But Wenner had a much better political sense than I did. He didn't need a weatherman to know which way the wind blew.

Why did you move to Mexico?

I moved to Mexico because I believe children come first and everything else is far down there on the priority list. Children come first here too. The things I saw in the commune terrified me (this was in 1970-71) and I decided that bad times were coming and it would be best to seek a safe haven.

I went back and forth over the years and then, when Reagan was elected, I was living in the penthouse at the Chelsea and people were living in the streets (something I had never seen in all my years as a kid in New York) and the subways were even more frightening than the commune.

One night in late 1980, I did a Candy Jones radio show to promote *The Journal of the Absurd* and a lady called in and asked me what I thought of Ronald Reagan. A spokesman for the arms industry, I replied charitably (I thought), who will bankrupt our economy in order to enrich a few Californian Nazis. *Oops.* This women just went bananas. I mean she was screaming in disbelief so bad that Candy had to cut her off.

During a long station break, Candy told me that after months of complaining about a gas leak, she was sitting in her apartment and the wall blew out and a man's head came flying into her living room, followed by a sheet of flame. She was miraculously still alive, but hadn't yet stopped trembling. Poor Candy. Beautiful, beautiful, beautiful. Won a lawsuit against the CIA (if I remember correctly) after having been drugged and used against her will in some kind of real-life spy drama.

On my way home, as I walked down Broadway to the nearest subway, two very evil-looking men braced me in a kind of dance trap and I thought, well

ANITA & ELI
Penrith Ranch, Newport, Wash., October 4, 1981
Photograph by Jules Siegel

this is it, why did I have to do this interview, why did I have to come back to New York and everybody has to go sometime, but they were just pimps trying to steer me to a not very attractive prostitute lurking nearby.

You get the picture. If you've been to Cancun, you know how different it is here, if very boring. Sometimes I feel as if I'm living in a minimum security prison. Seven to life in Cancun. It's like being married. Some days are heaven, some are hell, but when you look for an alternative.... I am hoping that being online will add some zest to my life.

What is your job at Playboy?

I don't work for *Playboy*. I'm a free-lance writer and I have done consulting work for them once in a while, such as recommending that they let the girls pick their own clothing, take pictures of them in their own homes and use natural light whenever possible.

To demonstrate what I meant, I showed Gary Cole, the photo editor some examples shot by Ron Thal of a red-headed, small busted, gray-eyed, Vassar weaver girl with paper-white skin I was then living with in an old mansion in Mendocino. She had a face right out of Botticelli.

He breathed deeply and he said, "I just wish I could use these pictures, Jules, but I have no strength for the fight it will entail."

I talk only to the top people there, who consider me a gifted imbecile, so these are not quite the insane ravings of a diseased mind, but pretty close.

Do you think it's really in your best interest to give facetious answers to serious questions?

Serious questions? Don't pull my leg. Go back to first question.

Aren't you a little old for this? I mean, really, 1935? You're actually over 60!

People are living longer and being more productive, too. Generally speaking, one generation serves as mentors for the next. Before the increase in life expectancy, older people were more highly valued for their knowledge and experience, because there were fewer of them. My generation, the Depression babies, were born in a low birth rate period, so we're pretty rare, too. Your question is a reflection of cultural lag.

Besides, how do you know that's really my age? In fact, how do you know this is really me? Virtual reality knows no boundaries of format or medium.

LA PALOMA & DE LA MADRID
Alameda de León, Oaxaca, Oax., 1982
Photograph by Jules Siegel

This was an illustration for a post card that I did for the Hotel Misión de los Angeles in the city of Oaxaca. "De La Madrid" refers to the President, whose campaign poster appears in the background. "*La Paloma*" is a play on his wife's name, Paloma, and the dove in the foreground. The card was printed as a false duotone of sepia and black from a zinc engraving with lead hand-type on a Heidelberg "Windmill" letterpress in a shop with a dirt floor.

The press is excellent, capable of printing four-color, but the cut was not the highest quality (to say the least), so I adapted my design to the technology and did an object that would easily have passed as antique were it not for the date on my copyright notice. I printed a couple of hundred extras and I sold them all in George Bennett's store in Puerto Escondido. They were a lifesaver on those endless days of no cash that were the routine for us until we moved to Cancun.

Fiction is the ultimate virtual reality. When you read a book the story appears in your mind and you lose contact with the outside world. I have been using HTML for exactly five days (as of the creation of this resumé). I'm a fast learner, but you should see my work in the media to which I have devoted my life — text, print and photography.

Hmm. What kind of a job are you looking for?

Something I can do from an Old People's Home without disturbing the other residents (except for my insane cackling as I score another howl of laughter). In other words, it's all done on the air—free-lance.

Travel?

It depends upon the remuneration and the motive.

What does "remuneration" mean?

We'll talk. Your guys will get together with my guys and crunch numbers. If that's not clear, go back to first question.

Index

A

amphetamines 34, 41–43
Anderson, Chester 104
Ann Arbor 87
Aphrodite 100–101
Army service 88

B

banana peels 17, 19,
  30, 113
Beach Boys 90
biodiversity 15, 17
Blaine, Diana York 62,
  66, 81, 106
Brown, Anita 23, 37, 56,
  69, 80, 97, 159, 161

C

Cady, Gardener 63, 78,
  125
Caesuras, David 20, 31
Cancun 66, 69
Cascadilla Hall 84
Cherdlu, Etienne 18, 30,
  31
Chrissie 29, 35–40,
  51–56, 58, 61–62,
  64–67, 70, 73–78,
  80–81, 90–91, 93–96,
  106, 118, 120
CIA 160
Clark, Craig 78
Cleanth, Siegel 83
Clinton, Bill 25, 26
Coley, Brett 25, 70
Cornell University 84,
  87–89, 111, 115
Crumb, Edward 56, 120

Crying of Lot 49, The 43,
  65, 71, 83, 91–92

D

davemarc 62, 105, 120
DeBus, Phyllis 89
Dinn, Andrew 9-10, 12,
  36, 44, 120
Dole, Bob 26
Don Martin 17
Donadio, Cadida 70
Donadio, Candida
  70, 92, 115
Dream, The 21
Dylan, Bob **45**, 90

E

Ebiri, Bilge 70-71
etaoin shrdlu 20

F

*Fear and Loathing in Las
  Vegas* 50
Forbidden Dreams 28
Friedman, Bruce Jay 112
Friedman, David Nevin
  18, 31

G

Genco, Dr. Robert 17
Glosup, Michael
  115, 120
Goddess, the 99–101
Gordon, Susan 52,
  84–85, 93
Gravity's Rainbow
  12, 14, 20, 23–24,
  41–44, 61–62, 65,
  68, 76, 81, 83, 91,
  97, 106, 111
Greek Myths 101
Grossman, Robert 33

H

Haberberger, George
  30, 50
hallucinogens 30
Holland, Brad 112
Humbert, Humbert 73
Hunter College 88-89

I

Ig Nobel Prize 14-15
Illustration America 112
Irving, Clifford 114

J

jazz 88
Jodorowski, Alejandro 76
Jones, Candy 160

K

Karatnytsky, Chris
  20-24, 57, 81
Kipen, David 26-27, 29
Kretchmer, Arthur
  29, 114
Kurzman, Harvey 56
Kyburz, Bonnie. L.
  99–100

L

Lament Del Cockroach
  14
Landgraben, Ellen 89
Laurel Canyon 51
Leucothea 100–101

Lineland 49
Lolita 73

M

M. Henry 51
Maas, Steve 66, 119
Maas, Steven 61
Mackin, Paul 30-31
Mad 17
Manhattan Beach
    51, 54, 92, 95, 115
marijuana 45, 139, 158
Martinez, Juan Cires 74
Mary 100-101
Mascaro, John 41-42,
    45-50, 61, 63, 82,
    106, 116, 148-151
Matthews, Robert 15
McLaughlin, Margot 14
Meikle, Jeff 114
Mexico *i-iv, xiv-xv*, 97-98
Mohanraj, Mary Anne *i*
Montalbano, Greg
    57, 110
Murphy, Paul 64

N

Nabokov, Vladimir
    71, 73
New York Times, The
    83, 94

O

Okamura, Chonosuke 15
Okamura Fossil Labora-
    tory 15, 17

P

Padgett, Penny 36-37,
    40, 41
Penthouse 42-43
People Magazine

55, *57, 62*, 119
Petersen, Arne Herley
    30, 51
Playboy 10, 29, 36, 41,
    56-58, 64-66, 73,
    94, 113-114, 162
Puzo, Mario 112
Pynchon family history
    85-86
Pynchon, John (brother)
    84
Pynchon, Judith (sister)
    84, 114
Pynchon, Mrs. (mother)
    84-85
Pynchon Plan 25-26
Pynchon, Thomas Sr.
    (father) 84-85, 115

R

Rice, Jeff 117-118
Rolling Stone 56
Romeo, Richard 18, 33

S

Samsel, Ted 31, 67
Saturday Evening Post 90
Schreiber, Brad 70
Siegel, Eli
    23, 69, 97, 158, 161
Siegel, Faera
    52, 69, 81, 97, 158
Siegel, Jesse 23, 97, 158
Siegel World Writing
    Industries *vi*, 9
Slothrop 21-22
Stanton, Tom 43, 54, 57,
    61-62, 104
Symmetra 14

T

teeth, Pynchon's
    insecurity with
    39, 64, 84, 85
tequila 158
Thal, Ron 80
Thill, Scott 64, 71
Thompson, Hunter S.
    50, 116
*Torn Shapes of Desire:
    Internet Erotica i*
Tumir, Vaskir 65

V

V. 12, 24, 39, 42, 43,
    65, 76, 83, 89, 91,
    99, 103, 104
Varo, Joe 51, 106-107
Velikovsky, Immanuel
    102, 104
Velvet Underground 31
Vineland 65, 97
Vosse, Michael 94

W

Wexler, Robert (Bob)
    35, 67, 69
Wexler, Christine.
    See Chrissie
White Goddess 101, 118
Who the Hell is Thomas
    Pynchon? i, 28-29
William Dean Howells
    Medal 83
William Faulkner Prize
    83
Wilson, Brian 91
Winograd, Terry 30

Y

Yenamandra, Murthy
    31, 110, 111